Riding
America's Backroads

Production Manager
Christa Neuhauser

Executive Editor
Heather Oliver

Editorial Director
James Parks

Researcher
Melanie Merritt

Contributors
Robert Annetzberger
Sanja Blagojevic
John Flores
Stanley Hansen
Troy Hendrick
Geoffrey Kula
Chris and Kathy Myers
Christian Neuhauser
James and Karen Parks
Robert Smith

Copy Editor
Bill Smith

Art Director
Gerald Müller

Riding American's Backroads is an original work, first published in 2009 by Fox Chapel Publishing Company, Inc.

ISBN 978-1-56523-479-6 (paperback)
ISBN 978-1-56523-481-9 (hardcover)

Library of Congress Cataloging-in-Publication Data

Riding America's backroads : 20 top motorcycle tours.

   p. cm. -- (The best of RoadRUNNER magazine)

ISBN: 978-1-56523-479-6 (pbk.) -- ISBN 978-1-56523-481-9 (hardcover)

1. Motorcycle touring--United States. 2. United States--Description and travel.
GV1059.52.R54 2009
796.70973--dc2

2009036185

To learn more about the other great books from Fox Chapel Publishing, or to find a retailer near you, call toll-free 800-457-9112 or visit us at *www.FoxChapelPublishing.com*.

Printed in China
First printing: November 2009

Riding
America's Backroads

20 Top Motorcycle Tours

An Assortment of Amazing Rides by

FOX CHAPEL
PUBLISHING

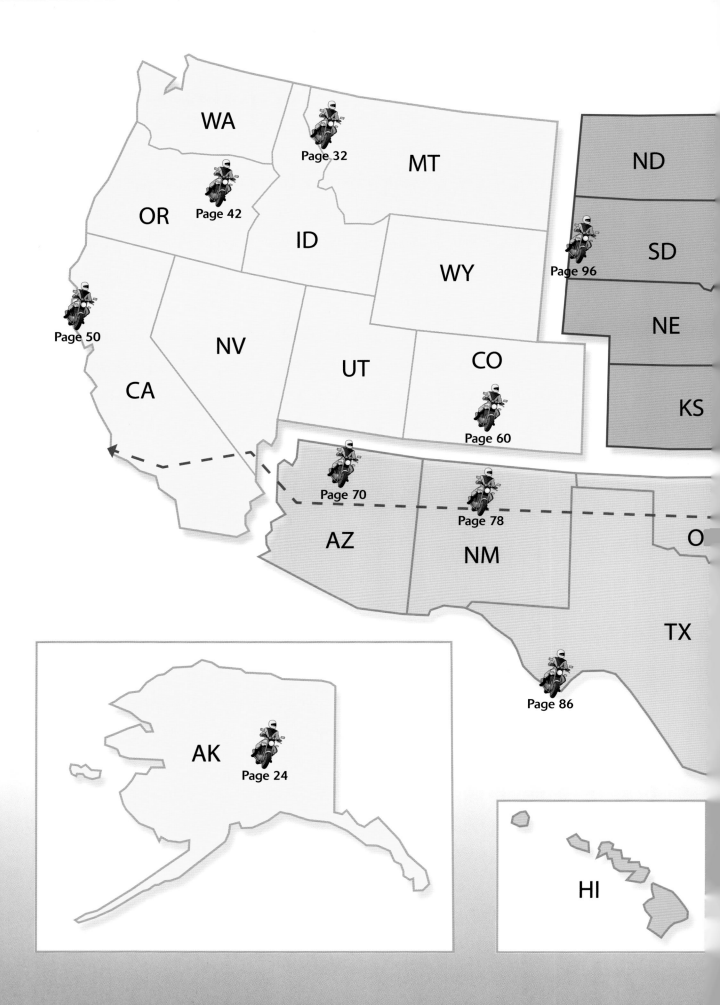

WA

Page 32

MT

ND

OR

Page 42

ID

SD

Page 96

WY

NE

Page 50

NV

UT

CO

KS

CA

Page 60

Page 70

Page 78

AZ

NM

O

TX

Page 86

AK

Page 24

HI

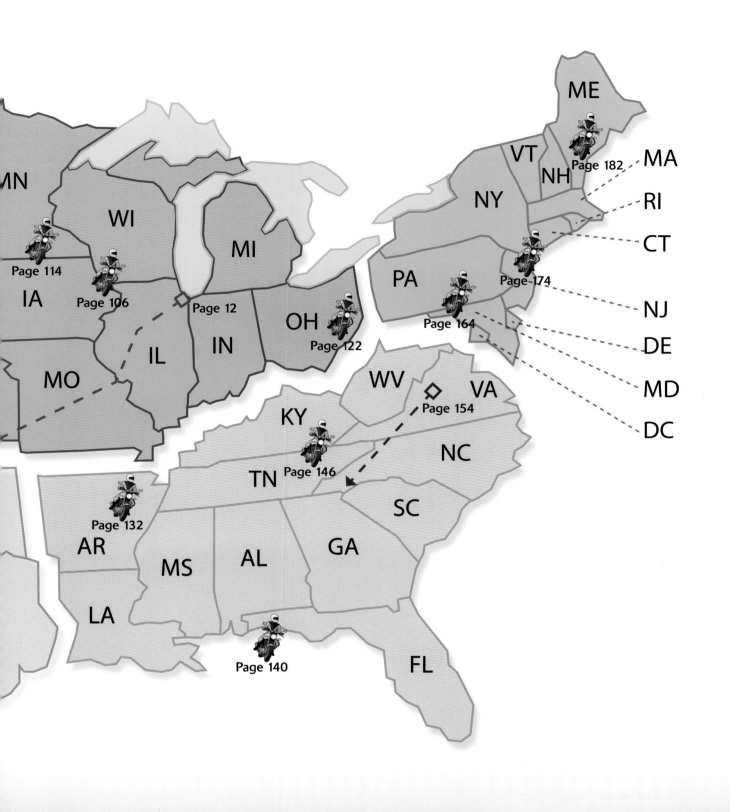

MN

ME

VT

NH

NY

MA

RI

CT

WI

MI

Page 114

IA

Page 106

Page 12

PA

NJ

DE

MD

DC

OH

Page 122

Page 174

Page 164

MO

IL

IN

WV

VA

Page 154

KY

NC

Page 146

TN

SC

Page 132

AR

AL

GA

MS

LA

FL

Page 140

- - - Cross Country Tour

Midwest

Northeast

West

Southwest

Southeast

Introduction

RoadRUNNER Motorcycle Touring & Travel magazine is a bi-monthly publication committed to experiencing the world on motorcycles. Our talented team of writers, photographers, and editors are dedicated motorcycle enthusiasts with years of on-road experience. We scout out interesting routes and research what to do and see along the way. The breathtaking scenery and memorable destinations discovered are captured in stunning photography and evocative touring articles.

Over the years, we've ridden countless roads and discovered scores of fascinating places to visit. There are so many extraordinary riding locations across the United States it was hard to select just 20 tours for this book, but we've done it, and we're confident you'll be pleased with the result. *Riding America's Backroads, Top 20 Motorcycle Tours,* is the first in a series of exciting books to come from *RoadRUNNER* magazine.

The *Facts and Information* section, at the end of each touring article, provides important logistical details for trip planning and a high level map. Riders should always consult more detailed maps when planning and taking these tours because our routes generally follow less-trafficked, secondary roads. GPS files and printable tank bag maps for each tour in this book can be downloaded at www.roadrunner.travel/ridingamerica. We've also included several service articles that cover various "how to" topics, including: trip planning, group riding, packing a bike and more.

Now, settle back in your favorite easy chair and let this book transport you along scenic backroads to exciting new places. We hope you will find our *Riding America's Backroads* to be both entertaining and an indispensable resource for planning your future trips. We've done the groundwork, it's time to go out and experience your own motorcycle touring adventures. Have fun, be safe, and enjoy the ride!

See you on the road,

Publisher of RoadRUNNER Magazine

Riding America's Backroads

Volume 1

Table of Contents

Cross Country Road Connector

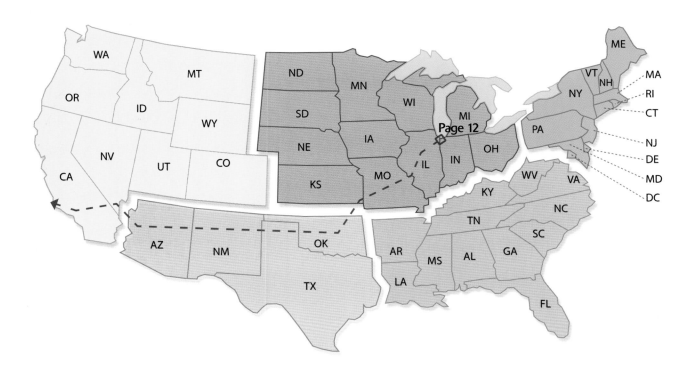

Life officially began for America's most famous cross-country route in 1926. John Steinbeck coined the road's nickname, "The Mother Road," in his 1939 book *The Grapes of Wrath*. The nickname stuck and has been synonymous with Route 66 to this day.

After World War II many motorists began following 66 to California, including a young troubadour named Bobby Troupe. The route inspired him to write the song "Get Your Kicks on Route 66," which became an instant hit. CBS added to the road's fame in the 1960s with the television series "Route 66" about two young vagabonds, Todd and Buzz, traveling cross-country in a Corvette.

The rapidly expanding Interstate Highway System, though, sounded the death knell for America's Mother Road, which was decommissioned in 1985. Although Route 66 is no longer an official US highway, its fame lives on. And today many travelers are still making the 2,500-mile trip from Chicago to LA along 66. Now, let's ride along with a young Austrian couple getting their kicks on Historic Route 66.

CALIFORNIA   ARIZONA   THE MOTHER ROAD   NEW MEXICO   Deep In

Main Street of America

today!

ALONG ROUTE 66
Getting More Kicks without the Corvette

You may know how it is. You're sitting through a long, cold winter evening beside the fireplace and dreaming about tours while the bike hibernates in the garage. Years ago I was in this situation. The fire crackled and Pink Floyd played in my headphones while I read an article about Route 66 in a motorcycle mag. The whole theme immediately captivated me and that very same evening, Christa and I began planning a vacation, our first in the States on a motorcycle.

↻ *Starting out on Route 66 in Illinois.*

"Fasten your seatbelts, please," the public address system blares. "We're landing in 30 minutes at Chicago's O'Hare International Airport." *Holy Moley, it's happening.* I'm nervous and hope my VN 1500 survived the trip. It's been sitting here, waiting on me for three days in Lufthansa's Chicago warehouse. Immigration goes smoothly and picking up the bike is a breeze. Interfracht did a great job and all I have to do is sign three sheets and we're on our way.

Illinois

Chicago welcomes us with all the friendliness imaginable. Easy immigration, fast processing when we pick up the bike, a deep blue sky above, temperatures in the 80s, and a smiling motorcycle cop waving for us to go faster. I do exactly 55 miles per hour, but that's too slow for the busybodies on Interstate 90. The flowing traffic carries us right downtown to a nice place to stay in the Holiday Inn close to Wacker Drive.

The next day we figure the best way to win the battle with jet lag is to set about exploring the city. But I'm not in the best of moods because I'm itching to get underway and roll on down the "Mother Road."

That journey starts the following morning. We begin as Tom Snyder's guidebook *Route 66 Traveler's Guide* says we should – at Mitchell's, a famous stop for 66 travelers heading west. The diner is packed and the waitress finally seats us. But of more concern to us than the menu choices is the thought that stop-and-go drudgery awaits us if all of these patrons choose to travel 66 simultaneously.

Christa takes her place on the backseat, and with the guidebook in her hands, she steers me through this huge city toward Joliet. It's easy to communicate through our half-shell helmets from Shoei. The real adventure has begun. First, Historic Route 66 matches up with 53 south. The Route 66 Association has marked the road very well, so it's easy to follow the right track. Soon it heads into a remote area and the road changes. Bumping along over cracks in the concrete, we pass dilapidated gas stations and grocery stores. Curves are a scarce commodity, but it doesn't matter because there is plenty to see. The only biker challenge is the varying surfaces. For a while, cobblestones in all shades of red bounce us to our lunch break at the Dixie Truckers Home, which includes a 66 museum, and there's no question whether we should stop or not. After a tremendous special something-something burger we roll on in the afternoon to our motel, the Carlin-Villa.

Missouri

Our second day on the road is only a short trip toward St. Louis. After approximately 240 miles into the tour, the "Gateway to the West" welcomes us. This 570-foot arch was built between 1959 – 1965 from the plans of architect Eero Saarinen. Inside the rust-free steel construction, the lift zips us to the top. I swear of all the towers and platforms I've stood upon, the experience at the apex of the Gateway Arch is the most breathtaking of all.

Today we take it easy. We only plan on riding 165 miles. After 94 miles we stop in Stanton to tour the Meramec Caverns, a complex of mineral formations with colors as rare and unique as they are beautiful. The caverns were used during the Civil War as a Federal powder mill and purportedly as a hideout for Jesse James. Situated in the lush foothills of Missouri's rolling Ozarks, these 400-million-year-old caverns hold fossils and

♠ *Real Route 66 charm: A rebuilt diner on exhibit at the highway museum in Texas.*

marvelous limestone formations of delicate stalactites and stalagmites. We take a well-guided tour through the world's largest cave formation, an eye-popping adventure that's open year round.

Back on 66 we discover the Devils Elbow. This part of Route 66 presents a challenge for drivers and cars during the winter and many have met their ends in accidents here. But it looks totally innocent now, with blue skies and green trees. We stop in Lebanon and, for only 27 bucks, check in at the Munger Moss Motel, an original Route

66 motel where we established a routine we never varied during the three weeks of our trip – unload the bike, jump in the pool, take a shower, and fill our empty stomachs.

Sunshine and a noisy truck wake us. I stretch my tired bones. "Cruisers aren't so comfy," I tell my groggy spouse. "I still prefer the tourer or sport touring bikes."

"Well, I can't complain," she replies, and I can understand why, with a sissy bar and our GIVI top case she can lean back and relax. Only today

↻ *Lou Mitchell's welcomes one and all 66ers.*

↻ *Almost as old as the road, a Texas gas station in the middle of nowhere.*

↻ *The snow-cap, one of the goofy cars in Seligman.*

↻ *Try stealing this 66 souvenir.*

In Oklahoma, Route 66 is an official highway and well maintained. In the morning we ride for El Reno, not knowing we had skipped by two gorgeous cities – Tulsa and Oklahoma City. The first break is taken in Sapulpa to visit a famous lady, Norma, as in Norma's Diamond Café. Norma, now in her early eighties, still works and her burgers and sandwiches are huge. The diner décor is authentic 1950s – '60s, and the jukebox only plays oldies.

Just 43 miles on, we turn to the left for our next stop in Stroud. An eye-catching Buick and the Rock Café attract my attention. And being outside in 99-degree heat is another good reason for a refreshing break. The owner is from Switzerland and it's quite a surprise for us to find a fellow German speaker in the town of Stroud.

In El Reno we check in at the Big 8 Motel, which advertises itself as Amarillo's Finest. *Texas?* I'm confused until I learn the sign is just a relic from the movie *Rain Man*. Just ask for room 117. That's where Dustin Hoffman and Tom Cruise "stayed."

Texas

The next morning before we cross into Texas, we stop in Clinton and walk through the very informative and tasteful Route 66 Museum. Exhibits from each decade of its existence document the colorful history of the "Mother Road" – from the tragic exodus of the Okies escaping the dustbowl in their over-loaded Model T Fords and their bloody welcome in California, to the wild, fun-loving sixties when a popular weekly television show portrayed Martin Milner and George Maharis in top-down adventures along the road.

When we arrive in Amarillo, 66 travels along a very rundown area and we have some problems finding a nice

she has bad luck. Bumpy roads and inches-wide cracks strain her spine and the suspension of my bike.

Oklahoma

Hot! Hot! Hot! Must stop, must stop. Christa gives me the thumbs up when I turn into the parking lot of an ice-cream parlor. The digital thermometer displays 104 degrees. Time for lemonade and ice cream. We overnight in Vinita and thoroughly enjoy the use of the pool.

motel. Finally we check in at the Navajo Inn. We adhere to our post-ride routine but can't find a restaurant. Burger King doesn't qualify; it had to do, however.

"Not what I expected in Texas, a rundown city and holes in the windows," Christa comments during our "opulent meal." We started to philosophize about Texas and decided that J.R Ewing and his clan had probably influenced our thinking much too unrealistically.

"Maybe we'll have more luck finding a nice sports bar," I suggest when we're back on the bike. We cruise down the empty road. Things don't look too promising, so I make a U-turn at the next intersection. Not a good idea. Blue lights flash in my mirrors and Christa starts teasing and taunting me. Officer Mendoza pulls us over.

↻ *Sadly, this relic of the Route dead ends.*

My thick accent and the Austrian license plate prove too much for Officer Mendoza. He calls for support and three minutes later a giant, at least 6'8" tall, shows up. I launch into the same story. He smiles.

"You're from Salzburg, right?" he guesses. "My granny is from Rosenheim and I was there a year ago. I stayed in Salzburg for a couple of days."

"Guys, you're crazy. You shouldn't stay around here. Shootings, drugs, and robberies are common occurrences every night. Pick up your stuff and I'll guide you to a good area. Otherwise I'll see you again tomorrow when you're reporting your stolen bike," he says.

Very sheepishly, we follow his advice and after so much excitement, we finally get to wind down and enjoy a beer in the bar at the Travelodge Inn. The next day my wife and I relax by the pool and recap our experiences of the last few days. There's no doubt the most outstanding event in our minds was meeting up with the helpful Officer Meyer.

New Mexico

"Nowhere in the world is the sky so blue as it is over Santa Rosa," Tom Snyder writes with certitude. But first we head towards Tucumcari, where we stop for a photo shoot around The Blue Swallow Motel, an excellent example of a dying landmark, the Route 66 motel. Back on the road we find Santa Rosa to check out the cerulean hues overhead. Tom is right. An overwhelming blue dome welcomes us and since we had finished our leg early, we checked in to our rooms with plenty of time left to float in the cool blue pool beneath that gorgeous sky.

○ *Arizona, passing zone.*

That night we hung out at Joseph's Bar and Grill. The food is delicious and reasonable. All of the other patrons show up in tight blue jeans, cowboy boots, checkered shirts, and cowboy hats. "It's Friday night," the bartender explains, "and all the guys bring their lady friends in from the farms for dinner and a dance." And even though Christa and I weren't about to try any of those hoedown steps, we certainly enjoyed being on-hand to witness the Western whirl of it all.

We roll across a very lonesome section of 66 the following day, and the road seems to have been made only for us, absolutely devoid of traffic except for one lone cowboy crossing on his horse. At the Pecos Pueblo, we're so caught up in the cultural experience of Indian ways that we lose all track of time. Afterward, the throttle gets a workout on the way to Santa Fe.

◑ *The Oatman Hotel: Gable and Lombard's honeymoon hideaway.*

There are so many motels and bed & breakfast possibilities to choose from here, that it makes for a difficult decision. But we find a cozy place near the center of town in an adobe motel. The El Rey Inn became our home for the next two days. And after covering 1,380 miles, we couldn't have picked a better spot for reinvigoration. The capital of New Mexico is quite distinctive in comparison to most other American towns. All the adobe structures, the outdoor marketplace, and the parks contribute to a completely relaxing experience. We strolled the galleries, lingered in coffee shops, and found a trove of small gifts made by Navajo craftsmen for our relatives in Austria.

Gallup is next on the list. But first we have to do two things. One, we have to drop in with other hungry roadies for the wonderful chili served in the 66 Diner at 1405 Central Avenue (a highly recommended eatery); and two, we have to make a stop at the Continental Divide. On the way we pass Cubero, familiar to many American Literature majors as the place where Ernest Hemingway settled in with his notebooks to write major portions of *The Old Man and the Sea*.

As dusk approaches, we arrive in Gallup. The deep, darkening colors of sunset and a huge neon sign for the El Rancho Hotel signals our travel day's end. We never found our accommodations anywhere else on our trip as easily. The hotel is a beautiful example of faithful restoration work and each of the rooms is tagged with the name of a Hollywood star who spent time here on location: Tracy and Hepburn, Bogart, Hayworth, Flynn, Gregory Peck and John Wayne. We were shown to the Hayworth Room, and later I fancied a melodramatic dance with Christa in the hotel bar.

Arizona

The sun blinks through the curtain and the warmth tickles my nose. Hitting the road, we soon cross the Petrified Forest National Park and take US 180 toward Holbrook. The ride through the forest is impressive and thought-provoking with all those eons spread before us.

We stop at Joe and Aggie's Café in Holbrook. It's two in the afternoon and we regret that we cannot rent one of the teepees in the Wigwam Motel (perhaps another day), but our target is still 91 miles away – Flagstaff, AZ.

The next day, we take an I-40 exit to Crookton Road, where a really wonderful stretch of Route 66 begins. We cruise on cracked, reddish asphalt towards Seligman and the wide-open spaces make the horizon look as though it's thousands of miles away. In Seligman we have to pause at Juan Delgadillo's wacky Snow Cap Drive-In. His brother Angel runs the barbershop in this town of 510 souls, and they both spearhead the local Route 66 preservation efforts.

After 172 miles under the burning Arizona sun, we arrive in Kingman. Exhausted and thirsty, we find the Travelodge Inn, check in, quench our pipes, and jump into the pool. Mr. D'z Diner fills the bill for dinner. Located on the site of the old Triangle Café, this 1950s-style eatery provides good food, a wonderfully kitschy interior, and sidewalk seating so you can watch the other Route 66ers.

We decided to wind up the tour in Needles before leaving 66 for the glitz of Las Vegas, after our long journey of 1,984 miles through flat farmland, lush valleys, the hills of the Ozarks, dustbowl terrain, the panhandle of Texas, and much of the Wild West.

↷ *And, believe it or not, with all the conveniences of home: Wigwams at the wayside.*

↷ *Adorable adobe abode.*

↷ *Route 66 No-tell Motel..*

Sandstone butte: A sure sign we're heading west.

San Gabriel Mountains, and discovered we were back on Route 66 in the middle of Santa Monica, CA. This story ought to have Route 66 ending at the Pacific Ocean, but it doesn't, just the way it should but doesn't begin on the shores of Lake Michigan.

Tom Snyder says, "Route 66 has always been a highway of fantasy" and we duly concur. I also truly appreciate his role in helping to fulfill this particular fantasy of mine, the one that sprang to life so long ago on a cold winter's night.

Oatman oasis.

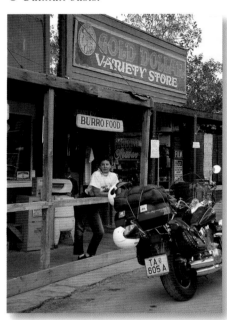

But first we discover Sitgreaves Pass and Oatman. We have used Tom Snyder's guidebook the whole tour and found his advice thus far to be right on the money. So, I'm shocked and disappointed after riding the great Sitgreaves Pass, which he compares to the most famous road in the Alps – the Passo Stelvio. Yes, I'll admit it features a few nice corners on the way to Oatman, but Mr. Snyder's boast is ridiculous. Sitgreaves Pass is a toddler's merry-go-round compared to the adrenaline-surging coaster of Passo Stelvio.

The main street in Oatman presents a funny mix of camera-burdened tourists, gun-toting locals, and the omnipresent burros. If you happen to stay awhile to explore the character of this old village, don't forget to check out the honeymoon hideaway used by Clark Gable and Carole Lombard – the Oatman Hotel.

In Needles, our Route 66 journey ends. Or, I should say, almost. Five days later, we survived an August crossing of Death Valley, ventured into the

They Do Drop In...again, and again.

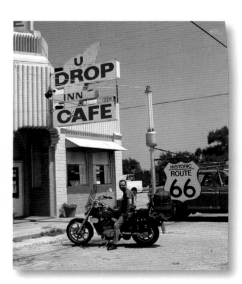

Along Route 66
FACTS AND INFORMATION

Total Mileage

Approximately 2,679 miles.

In General

Traveling Route 66 is a special experience along a byway that chronicles big chunks of American history. Once traversed as the National Old Trails Highway, this diagonal course was built to link hundreds of rural towns with cosmopolitan centers, and though much displaced today by the Interstate Highway System that President Eisenhower initiated, it still presents a colorful tableau of cafes, motels, gas stations, tourist attractions and vivid architectural styles from many decades. Every state along the way has its own R66 association to erect historical markers and signs (often stolen as souvenirs) and to help maintain the parts of R66 that survive.

Travel Season

If you do the entire road in one piece, we recommend traveling between April and October. The different climate zones are a consideration, too. In April it's still cold in Illinois and probably much too hot in the Mojave Desert.

Roads & Biking

Cobblestones, asphalt, and old concrete will challenge you the entire tour and finding the right directions isn't always easy. In some areas, 66 is only a service road for I-40, or worse it's broken up with dead ends. Watch for the brown historical road signs and you won't get lost too often. Curves are rare. Cruising bikes, tourers, or big enduros ought to be the right picks for tripping down Route 66.

Books & Maps

○ *Here It Is! The Route 66 Map Series*
Ghost Town Press
ISBN 0967748143, $11.75
○ *Route 66: Traveler's Guide and Roadside Companion*
by Tom Snyder, Macmillan
ISBN 0312254172, $13.95

More Information

○ National Historic Route 66 Federation
www.national66.com
www.historic66.com
○ Oklahoma Route 66 Museum
www.route66.org
○ Petrified Forest & National Park
www.nps.gov/pefo

Attractions

❶ Sears Tower Skydeck
(312) 875-9447
❷ Route 66 Hall of Fame & Museum
(815) 844-4566
❸ The Lincoln Home
(217) 492-4241
❹ Lou Mitchell's Restaurant & Bakery
(312) 939-3111
❺ Petrified Forest & National Park
(928) 524-6228
❻ Oklahoma Route 66 Museum
(580) 323-7866
❼ Gillioz Theatre, (417) 863-9491
❽ Blue Whale Roadside Attraction
(405) 258-0008
❾ Santa Monica Pier
(310) 458-8901

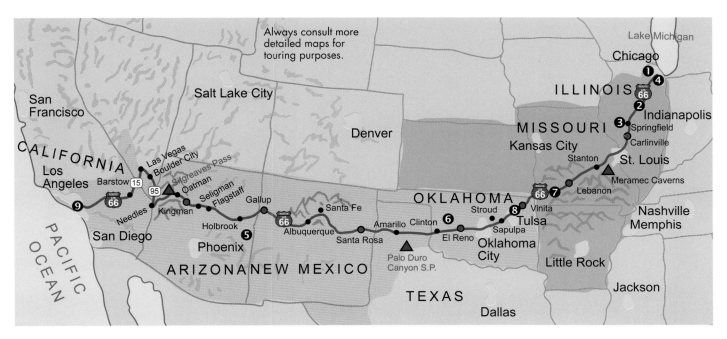

The West

The American West has been immortalized in music, literature, film, art, and in countless other ways. But the best way to experience it is from the open road. The National Parks found in Utah, Wyoming, Montana, California, Oregon, Washington and Alaska are an extraordinary collection of natural wonders.

There is a veritable mother lode of iconic byways to explore, including the tranquil meanderings of the Pacific Coast Highway, magnificent vistas of The Going to the Sun Road in Glacier National Park, the dizzying heights of the San Juan Skyway, stark beauty along the Death Valley Scenic Byway, breathtaking views from the Historic Columbia River Highway and many more.

From the glitz of Las Vegas and Los Angeles to the towns in Montana, Wyoming and Idaho that still recall the Old West to the farming communities in California's Central Valley and on to the posh ski resorts of Utah and Colorado, the region is a sea of contrasting cultures and lifestyles. Pack your saddlebags, friend, because we're off to see the West.

ALASKA
THE NORTHERN EXPEDITION TOUR

Tired, I stumbled into the airplane. Heading for Seattle on a BMW K 1200 GT, I had left Spokane at five o'clock in the morning. Four hours later, I spotted the city skyline, made for the airport and eventually fell into my seat totally worn out. Only a buzz of excitement about seeing Alaska could keep me awake. Our Boeing takes off. Seattle, the ocean and the many islands disappear behind a white curtain of cloud. And in a sense, so did I. The next thing I know, a flight attendant announces our landing in Anchorage. I had slept the entire flight.

Text and Photography: Christian Neuhauser

↻ *A pond and picturesque mountains along the Dalton Highway.*

↻ *Our cabin in Talkeetna on Petersville Road.*

↻ *The "Freeman Squadron" on the Dalton Highway.*

"What's going on in the lower forty-eight?" Phil Freeman asks, welcoming me to Alaska. "I don't know," I say. "I've been scouring the roads in Oregon and Washington for the last three weeks, so I wouldn't have a clue about the other 46."

This first night I'm on my own. I will be exploring Alaska with Phil and a group of riders. But I don't have to look very far for company and a good time. Gwennie's, a nice restaurant and bar, is right across from the Days Inn, and it's just the spot for the locals and lonesome tourists to meet. At the bar, Joe, a local Harley rider, tells me about his three years in Australia and New Zealand and how much he'd like to return. He's definitely a character and I enjoy exterminating a few tankards of beer with him before walking back to the hotel. No problem finding the way – it is still light out at 2:30 a.m.

The next day I pick up my boon companion for the days that follow, a Kawasaki KLR 650. Phil tells me a bit about the surrounding areas and gives me directions to Girdwood, where we're scheduled to meet the other riders in the evening. Then, I'm off to familiarize myself with the Kawi while exploring Anchorage and nearby back roads. The weather is dreary, overcast. Now and then, sprinkles fall from the deep gray folds of hanging clouds. Discovering some gravel roads, I soon gain experience with Alaskan drivers and have to hone my avoidance techniques when a number of cars and trucks, wildly careening and spraying grit along the route, attempt to cut me off. It doesn't take long for me to get my fill of their behavior – and the rocks, dirt and mud – before turning and burning my way to Girdwood.

That evening, I meet up with my riding buddies, the other members of our northern expedition. Bill and Ed, from Bloomfield, Michigan, are all about Harleys back home, a fact that I might have deduced from Bill's footwear. He's wearing Timberland boots and white socks. All in good fun, breaking the ice, I ask him when highly visible, "whiter than white" socks had become mandatory safety gear for riders in Michigan. He laughs. Dave from Maryville, TN, and Johnny from Abingdon, VA, live closer to my base in Clemmons, NC, and being so far away, it sounds good, like *home*, whenever they drawl a y'all (as in "How y'all doing?") in conversations. Last on the list, but not least, the international rep in the group is Nigel, from England. But he is quick to correct that territorial impression. "I'm from Wales and I live in Scotland. I only work in England," he emphasizes.

Our base for the next two nights, the Alyeska Winner Creek B&B in Girdwood is a beautiful lodge-style log home designed and built in 1997 by our hosts Victor and Kim Duncan. A terrific spot, and you couldn't ask for better breakfasts.

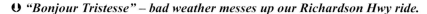
↻ *"Bonjour Tristesse" – bad weather messes up our Richardson Hwy ride.*

Tour Diary

Monday, July 19 – We start out with a little warm-up loop to Seward and back. The scenery would be magnificent, but we see only cloud-covered mountains. At least it isn't raining. From time to time, the clouds disappear and we spot the Chugach Range. The outlook improves in the center of the Kenai Peninsula, and it makes sense for us to branch off on a side trip to Hope, a little fisherman's village on Cook Inlet.

Tuesday, July 20 – We leave our lovely, cozy place in Girdwood. The sky is gray-on-gray and sometimes raindrops hit my visor. We head toward Palmer on Glenn Highway. Just north of Palmer, the ride jogs west for a wilderness detour to Hatcher Pass. About 10 miles up Palmer-Fishhook Road, where the pavement gives way to gravel, the road enters a gorge. The brownish ribbon of pavement sneaks smoothly through the stands of willow, spruce and birch that border the Little Susitna River. It once yielded gold, but now it is prized for silver – silver salmon, that is.

↺ *Exploring the grandeur near Girdwood.*

After a pleasant, more challenging ride, we arrive at the Hatcher Pass Lodge. Nestled above the heart of the Mat-Su and Susitna Valleys, the lodge serves as a springboard for travelers who come to explore a world of stunning mountain vistas. From time to time, when the gray veil lightens and almost parts, I imagine how breathtaking this high tundra of alpine lakes and meadows with wildflowers in bloom can be in bright sunlight. The spot is an outdoor mecca for mountain bikers and hikers, and even a dual-sport rider could find his bliss here. I do.

After a delicious lunch, I swing through three big sweepers and stop to stand on top of Hatcher Pass (elevation 3,886ft.). My timing is perfect. The sky clears briefly to afford a view of the Talkeetna Mountains as clouds boil over the crest and drift into the valley. The sun blinks through and disappears again. This play of gathering light, then darkness, goes on and on.

○ *Amusing Alaskan advertising: We got breakfast.*

We arrive in the picturesque village of Talkeetna. This colorful town is the base for expeditions to Mt. McKinley, North America's loftiest pinnacle (20,320ft.). Tonight, we shelter at Gate Creek Cabins in Trapper Creek, where we replenish with freshly grilled steaks.

Wednesday, July 21 – We explore Petersville Road before stopping for breakfast at Forks Roadhouse. This road is the first real challenging ride of our trip. A tight, potholed stretch of back road, it's got some hairy turns, too. The afternoon is a relaxing ride to Nenana. A little side trip meanders in and out of Denali National Park. Visitors wishing to explore further and see specimens of the stunning varieties of wildlife living in the heart of the park must travel there by bus. But since it's too late in the day for any of us to go, we continue to our overnight stop. Nigel, David and I hit the one and only bar in town and wound up considering who the best musicians in the world are until well into the morning.

Thursday, July 22 – The short night wasn't too bad. Up and about, in short order we arrive in Fairbanks where Dave and I stroll around and find a good place for some coffee and pastry. This is the last glimpse of real civilization we'll see for a while. In the afternoon, the Dalton Highway becomes our home for the next five days. The pavement ends at the intersection with Elliott Highway, but there's a paved part between Fox and Livengood that presents a chance for me to spur the KLR through a series of wide sweepers. Soon my companions have vanished in the rearview. Only Nigel follows me later. The unpaved section is a lot of fun: great sweepers and nice, tighter turns combined with a high-speed stretch. The KLR isn't the only one loving this terrain. I'm a full hour ahead of the others when reaching our rendezvous north of the Yukon River.

○ *Gold diggers and mud hoppers "cap" off their mornings in Forks Roadhouse with breakfast.*

⤷ *I made it! The Arctic Circle.*

Friday, July 23 to Monday, July 26 – We stay on the Dalton Highway.

Like a crystal-clear tent, blue arches across the sky when we arrive at the landmark 66°33″: The Arctic Circle. Cameras come out to preserve for all posterity the images of another brave band of explorers standing beside the big wooden sign that marks the spot. Everyone is taking shots and changing places to pose for their family albums. Meanwhile, the mosquitoes are eating us up.

I return to the road earlier than the rest to take advantage of the perfect light for photography. I'm having a blast – everything is going right today and I'm in the best of moods. Elated, I fly toward Coldfoot.

The next day we explore Atigun Valley and Atigun Pass. The weather shows its best side and we have a great time. The road is a smooth run through the valley before it climbs 4,739 feet to Atigun Pass. Back near Coldfoot, Dave, Johnny, Nigel and I stage a little private race. Opening the throttles, we zip back to our hotel as though we're competing in the Paris-Dakar Rally.

Changing the plans for the day, we decide to ride to Prudhoe Bay. Even though it means doing the Atigun Pass again, the idea is roundly welcomed. It also means 240 miles of dust and economical riding. There isn't one gas station between Coldfoot and Prudhoe Bay. Plenty of oil but no gas.

We leave Coldfoot at 8:30 on the dot for the big journey to the northernmost place anyone can reach in the USA on a public road, and we spot our first bear right before Atigun Pass. A grizzly, he sits close to the road, enjoying some quiet time in the morning sun.

⋔ *Great glacier vistas in the southern Chugach Mountains.*

Of course, we stop, motors running, and try to take pictures, but the bear isn't having anything to do with that: He stands, turns, and shows his great behind. Later, on Atigun Pass, a handful of Dall sheep cross the road. A nice experience: Days have gone by without any wildlife sightings. Now they're coming out of the woods in the space of an hour as though our tires were baited.

Crossing over the Brooks Range and riding toward Prudhoe Bay is enough to demonstrate for me how big Alaska is. It seems I ride forever without making miles. I pass Galbraith Lake and Tool-ik Lake, two sapphire-blue relics from

the glacial ages. At the Coastal Plain Overlook, I stop to admire the view over the tundra, which is so expansive, so panoramic, I'm convinced I can see the curvature of the earth. Honestly, I cannot describe the feeling I have here. Once again, planet earth has shown me very clearly how small we humans are. Awesome! Thirty-seven miles later, I arrive in Deadhorse at the Caribou Inn. A short excursion to the Arctic Sea ends the day.

Same road, another day: You might think that's boring and you'd be so wrong. Coming at these spectacular vistas from the other side, I'm just as

○ Hatcher Pass is challenging.

interested and inspired. Some of us leave earlier to take advantage of the morning light and the small fog banks crawling by. The rest of the crew catches up eventually and we all ride back to Coldfoot together.

Tuesday, July 27 – Back on the Dalton Highway towards Nenana. Much like yesterday: the same road and flipside scenery that's just as beautiful.

Wednesday, July 28 – Still on the Dalton Highway for 57 miles. There, we have a chance to veer from semi-familiar terrain and satisfy our curiosity about the Elliott Highway, the road to our next overnight, the Manley Roadhouse. The town of Manley is home to 72 people and still maintains the gritty charm of the last frontier. Before arriving, we take a challenging off-road passage toward the Yukon River. Unfortunately, the last couple of miles aren't doable, due to deep mud that's dangerous without the right tires. So, we turn back to the Elliott Highway. This side trip is exhausting, and Michigan Ed knows it, yelling out when he finally opens his visor, "Oh, yeah! I'm the enduro man!"

Our dinner is rich, and wanting to get it properly settled, we decide to have a few rounds before we listen to our pillows. Bob shows up and tells us his life story. He has owned the Manley Roadhouse for 33 years and also serves as the township's full-time postmaster. All of his other tales could fill a fat space on a library shelf.

Thursday, July 29 – After a few great days, we have a real dreary time of it heading toward Delta Junction. The one highlight today is the moose I spot.

Friday, July 30 – Promises to be a gorgeous ride on the Denali Highway. We take Hwy 4 toward Paxson in the morning. After passing a pretty palette of wildflowers, grazing caribou, a peak called Donnelly Dome, and a retreating glacier that once nearly engulfed the road, the Richardson Highway reaches its highest point, 3,000 feet, at Isabel Pass. The route skirts scenic wild lands, lakes and free-flowing rivers. I take a right on the Denali Highway, open the throttle and goad the KLR through the wide sweepers towards Lake Summit. Later, I cross MacLaren Summit (4,085ft.), the second-highest highway pass on the Alaskan road system.

Today's destination is Gracious House, but before our arrival, Phil shows us another great road that peters out and ends in the middle of the wilderness. River crossings, deep potholes, mud, gravel and dirt are all arrayed to challenge riders and bikes.

Tomorrow there are a few miles of gravel left before we head back to Anchorage, the end of the tour. Exploring here was a once in a lifetime experience. And Alaska's amazing scenery is matched only by the camaraderie and fun had while riding this motorcycling mecca.

○ Stretching my legs at the Finger Mountain Overlook.

FACTS AND INFORMATION

Total Mileage
Approximately 1,669 miles.

In General
Alaska is a wonderful place to be, the state for outdoor activities. And, for motorcycle enthusiasts, Alaska offers exciting roads. But unlike the situation in other states, it is tough to plan round trips in Alaska because the road system is mostly based on cul-de-sacs. Traffic ranges from very light to usually nonexistent. Only along the pipeline from Prudhoe Bay toward Valdez does one expect heavy truck traffic. For first timers, we recommend going with a tour operator. In many areas you are cut off from civilization. Certain varieties of wildlife (curious bears, loose moose!) may present unwelcome circumstances for anyone going alone.

Travel Season
The best time of the year to go is between May and August. GORE-TEX® riding gear might be the best choice and, very important, take a pair of waterproof boots.

Roads & Biking
Lots of great paved roads and challenging dirt-and-gravel roads to spoil you. The scenery is breathtaking. To explore and experience all the corners, dual sport bikes are the best choice.

Food & Lodging
Anchorage and Girdwood have some nice but very expensive restaurants. The quality is good to excellent. It's a different story in the rest of the state: simple food at high prices, with the exception of restaurants on the Denali Highway.

Lodging north of the Yukon River is simple. Full of character, the most unique place we stayed was the Manley Roadhouse.

Maps
- *Rand McNally Easy to Read! Alaska State Map*
  by Rand McNally and Company
  ISBN 978-0528875847, $4.95
- *Alaska Atlas and Gazetteer*
  by DeLorme Publishing,
  ISBN 978-0899332895, $19.95

More Information
- State of Alaska Travel and Vacation
  www.travelalaska.com
- Alaska Wildlife Adventures
  www.alaskawildland.com
- Alaska Restaurant Guide
  alaska.usn.myareaguide.com/restaurants.html
- Fairbanks Convention & Visitors Bureau
  www.explorefairbanks.com
- Anchorage Convention & Visitors Bureau
  www.anchorage.net
- Dalton Highway
  www.blm.gov/ak/dalton

Attractions
❶ Alaska Native Heritage Center
(800) 315-6608
❷ Fairbanks Ice Museum
(907) 451-8222
❸ Northern Lights: the Aurora Borealis Ester Dome
(907) 479-2500
❹ Arctic Circle Tours
Northern Alaska Tour Company
(907) 474-8600
❺ Riverboat Discovery
(907) 479-6673
❻ 26 Glacier Cruise by Phillips Cruises
(907) 276-8023
❼ Kenai Fjords National Park
(907) 224-7500

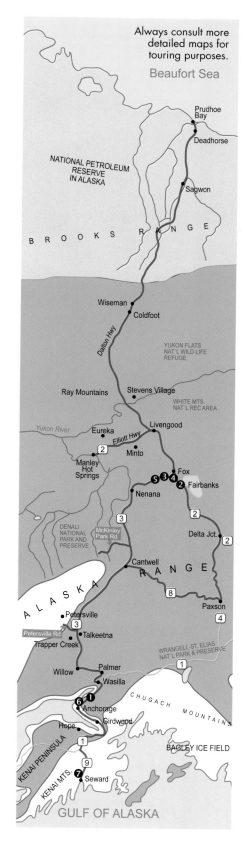

Always consult more detailed maps for touring purposes.

Shamrock Tour® – Kalispell, Montana

"Going to the sun..."

Sprawled just north of Flathead Lake in northwest Montana, Kalispell is a terrific spot for a shamrock base. To the east, you have the magnificent Rockies and Glacier National Park; north and west, the rambling peaks of the Salish and Cabinet Ranges; and then the 28-by-15-mile lake and the Mission Range to the south. Mountains, lakes, and great roads – what's not to like? Four days, four leaves of the Shamrock.

Text and Photography: Robert Smith

⋒ *Goggles help Tribble watch the road.*

⋒ *Climbing through the forest toward Yaak Summit.*

↺ *Gil Mangels shows off the Miracle of America Museum's latest acquisition.*

Tour 1: "To Yaak and Back"

A saying in these parts, "to Yaak and back," means a long journey, although Yaak is less than 100 miles from Kalispell. I'm meeting Skip, Maggie and Sasha at the Buffalo Café in Whitefish for breakfast, but what we've all forgotten is, it's Labor Day. The Buffalo is closed, and we have to relocate to another eatery around the corner.

Mike arrives, as do Eric, Annabelle, and Tribble, a speed-crazed Yorkshire terrier. "He used to duck his head inside the tank bag whenever we went over 40," says Eric. "So we got him the goggles."

We're six bikes heading north on US 93 to Trego though Sasha has to turn his magnificent Vincent for home. Highway 93 is a mostly straight two-laner running to the Canadian border, but at Trego, we turn west on Montana 353, and the difference is dramatic. The narrow, bumpy pavement heads off into dense forest, climbing into the Salish Mountains. This is logging country and the tires of overladen trucks have hammered deep troughs into the tarmac. Maggie and Eric/Annabelle/Tribble lead the way, both riding R 1150 GS Adventures, which float over the undulations. Mike's Guzzi and Skip's Ducati shudder and lurch over the tarmac ripples while I bounce along behind on my Sprint ST.

"Lucky it's a holiday," says Mike when we pull into the Libby Dam Visitor Center to expel some of our breakfast coffee. "No log trucks." These roads can be deadly on weekdays. The truck drivers are mostly self-employed and paid by the load. Motorcycles are just speed bumps to them…

Instead of following the dam access road north, we turn west toward Libby, splitting north on Montana 567 just before the US 2 intersection. Warm sunlight filters through the tall evergreens that tower over the road as we wind uphill.

This would be a fast road but for the surface, beaten by trucks and split by frost heaves. It's a real workout trying to stay with the two GSs through the undulating corners, but I can catch them on the short straights. The incline flattens and the road straightens as Yaak's nearly famous Dirty Shame Saloon comes into view. The only other edifice is a general store in shambles. Yaak, we discover, is a Kootenai Indian word for arrow; and the town is named after the Yaak River, which cuts through their territory just like one.

Inside, the walls of the ramshackle Dirty Shame are lined with banknotes, and the clientele eye us coolly, especially when we order Pepsis and water. They're welcome to think what they will, but we know bikes and beers don't mix.

From Yaak, Montana 337 takes us east, skirting steep, wooded hillsides and precipitous cliffs. We break through the trees at Yaak Summit and look out over a glorious valley of dark conifers. Here, the clear-cuts are much less evident than the carnage in Canada's Kootenay Mountains to the north. From here, 337 snakes down through the valley to Lake Koocanusa, a steep-sided blue-water basin longer than the horizon.

And on the road from Rexford to Eureka, I learn the answer to a question that's been bugging me since I got here. All the white-painted metal crosses at the roadside, obviously indicating road fatalities, are part of a statewide, accident reduction program organized by the Lions Club. Timely reminders…

The others having dispersed, Skip, Mike and I wash down the day's throat dust with a cold one beside the shimmering waters of Stillwater Lake. A grand day out.

Tour 2: Mist Opportunities

I know something's not right when I step outside the hotel the next morning to find the Sprint covered in white ash. The wind has swung round, bringing in smoke from forest fires burning to the northeast, and there's an acrid taste in the hazy air. I point the Triumph west, downwind, on US 2, hoping to outrun the smoke, but the whole region is draped. I pull off at McGregor Lake to take some snaps, but smoke obscures it like dense fog.

I pause at a gas station in Libby to fuel up for the ride through the Cabinet Mountains. An archetypal lumber town, Libby has two distinguishing features: a massive statue of an eagle dominating the eastern approach, and that endangered American icon, a drive-in movie theater. Montana 56 turns south just before Troy, and the broad two-laner winds lazily toward the distant hazy humps of the Cabinets. It's a recreation access corridor, and the road is lined with RV parks, private lakeside properties and fishing stores. Further south, these fade out as I leave the lakes behind, but the mountains never seem to get closer, shrouded as they are in their smoky brown blanket.

Montana 200 picks up 56 just before Noxon on the Flathead River, and I try some more photography across the water at Trout Creek. I can just make out the massive escarpment of Flat Iron Ridge as it tumbles to the roadside above the river near Thompson Falls, but so much of it is just haze.

Then just before Plains (or Wild Horse Plains, to give its full name) a yard full of colorful cement ornaments catches my eye. The "Closed" sign is out and I'm peering over the fence when Bill Haun appears. Seventy something, rail thin, and missing teeth, Bill invites me in. "Want a beer? I'm having one." Not when I'm riding. Bill then tells me his life story, especially the saga of his cement lawn-ornament business and the many franchises it's spawned. "I don't charge them," he says. In spite of myself, I can't resist snapping shots of Bill's motor-

↻ *Forest roads are a great playground for the R 1150 GS.*

cycle-riding cement pigs, although I pass on some of his saucier creations.

North from Plains, Montana 28 takes me across the Flathead Reservation, a vast, golden grassland sea, and toward one of my favorite views: the western approach to Flathead Lake at Elmo. Alas, like most of the day, the lake is lost in smoke.

Tour 3: American Miracle

I've arranged to meet Maggie at the Miracle of America Museum in Polson, at the south end of Flathead Lake. Her friend, Gil Mangels, the proprietor and curator, has promised me the inaugural firing of a 1931 Scott the museum has just acquired. I choose the west side of Flathead Lake for the one-hour journey south. Unlike the eastern shore, which is lined with private

⌒*Bill Haun with his cement biker pigs.*

↻ *The Going to the Sun route overlooks Avalanche Creek.*

◐ *Flathead Lake is best seen from its western side.*

homes obscuring the view, this shoreline has contours that are more interesting and it's mostly accessible from the road.

US 93 hugs the lakeside, deeking around the numerous points and inlets, and the smoke haze still hangs on the

↻ *Sasha's magnificent Vincent Shadow waits outside the Buffalo Cafe in Whitefish.*

lake. Normally it would be a brilliant crystal blue under clear sun, but el sol, struggling to break through the haze, fails to moderate the early morning chill, and when I meet Maggie in the parking lot of the MOAM, I'm quite cold.

The Museum is Gil's lifetime collection of machinery, equipment, household goods, mementoes, bric-a-brac and period ephemera. Unbelievers might use the j-word, but Gil has assembled a fascinating assortment of "nostalgiana" grouped into general themes: military vehicles, motorcycles, bicycles, radios, clothing, appliances, tools, farm machinery and on and on. In the foyer, I meet Gil's wife, Joanne, who seems quite unfazed by the enormity of the collection. Any of the guys I know who have amassed even a twentieth of Gil's Augean stable of stuff are either single or long divorced. As one TV channel says, a day at the Museum would be "time well wasted."

And so to the Scott. Recently donated by The Antique Motorcycle Club of America director, Gary Breylinger, the two-stroke twin is based on a 1908 design by Alfred Angus Scott. Isle of Man TT winners in 1912-13, Scotts were advanced machines in their early days but failed to progress, especially after Alfred Scott left the company in 1915. Gil and I spend about 20 minutes toying with the Scott's unfamiliar levers, cables and switches, but our kick-starting attempts all meet with failure. A phone call to Gary for tips, more uneducated guesswork with the controls, and a push start finally bring the Scott burbling to life. Gil chugs around the museum's backyard and struggles with the Scott's two-speed gearshift. There are lots more motorcycles in the collection, including a gorgeous Model 7 Sunbeam sidecar outfit and a Norton flat-tracker. But it's time for me to get going…

South of Polson on 93 is the National Bison Range, a grassland refuge for the lumbering beasts who gaze unconcerned as trucks rumble by. Continuing south to Missoula, the road is a heavily trafficked highway, as is 200 east to the Montana 83 turnoff. Though technically undemanding, I enjoy the relative calm of 83's almost nonexistent traffic

◑ *...and just as dramatic on the eastern approach.*

and gentle hills. The road effectively follows the Rocky Mountain trench, a parallel trough just west of the foothills. The Rockies are obscured by the Flathead National Forest – and the ever-present pall of forest fire smoke. Twice there's a hold up at firefighting access points on the road: helicopters, trucks and tenders wait while weary crews

◑ *Views from the west side of Logan Pass are magnificent...*

eat at makeshift camps surrounded by tents and mobile washrooms.

For a change of pace, I pull off the road to investigate the town of Bigfork. Parked on its spruced and tidy main street is a Willys Jeepster, the civilian version of the WWII General Purpose transport. I'm just taking a picture of the shiny red ragtop when its owner appears:

"Triumph, eh? I've got a '69."
"I've got a '70," I fire back.
"I've got a 1927 Scott, too."
"I was just looking at a Scott today."
"At the museum?"
"Yes."
"I sold that to Gil."
"Then you must be Gary."
He is.

Tour 4: Going to the sun

Mike and Skip have volunteered to ride with me on their Nortons to make the next day's photo shoot more interesting, but the air quality is the worst yet, "hazardous" is the word used on the weather report. We ride east on US 2 through Columbia Falls to West Glacier

and the park entrance, turning north to Lake McDonald. But visibility deteriorates: Most of the forest fires are in the park itself, and even staying in visual contact with the other bikes isn't easy. With no chance of any decent photography, Mike and Skip head home, but Maggie and I decide to continue. The Going to the Sun Road is a spectacular ride, even in the gloom. Sheer walls of rock rise into the smoke above the narrow winding highway, while a low stone wall is all that prevents hapless excursions into the steep valley below. It's occurred to me many times that the "safety" barriers designed for cars are actually dangerous to bikers. Though it might halt a four-wheeler, making contact with the stone barrier on the Going to the Sun Road would pitch a bike and rider into oblivion.

The air is better at Logan Pass, upwind of the worst blazes, but the massive tors and peaks surrounding the pass are impenetrably hazy. At St. Mary on the east side of the pass, the air is clear but the scenery mundane. We decide to take Montana 49 to East Glacier instead of the longer route through Browning. It's a good idea: the road swings south in a seemingly endless succession of beautiful curves. From Kiowa, the surface is less well maintained and the terrain more challenging. We sprint over open ranchland as the tarmac bobs and weaves over undulating hillocks and along barren ridges. The surface convulses with ripples, and gravel makes occasional incursions. Cattle graze at the roadside. "It's a Crackerjack road," Maggie quips. "There's a surprise round every corner."

We stop for a drink at the Isaak Walton Inn, a beautiful century-old lodge in Essex, near Marias Pass. John F. Stevens of the Great Northern Pacific Railroad named the pass after his niece. I decide I have to return to the Park for another try. The scenery at Logan Pass looked so promising in the smoky gloom.

Tour 4: Reprise

I'm lucky to get an extra day en route from Salt Lake City to Portland, Oregon, a week later. The fires are under control, and the day promises sunshine. I meet Maggie for breakfast in Bigfork, and we spin north into the Park. This time the air is clear and the meaning of "Going to the Sun" more obvious. Cut into the cliff side, the road climbs ever upward toward Logan Pass, faithfully following the contours of the rock face. The geography, more vertical than horizontal, is like a world turned on its side. At the pass, the ridges and peaks soar skyward, dwarfing the visitor center and parking lot. To the east, the craggy peaks and lush valleys almost look too real to be true, like a studio backdrop.

Montana is famous for its Big Sky and now, thanks to the firefighters, I've finally seen it.

◗ *The beautiful blue of Lake Koocanusa.*

Kalispell, Montana
FACTS AND INFORMATION

Total Mileage

Approximately 1,040 miles.

In General

Kalispell sits in the Flathead Valley, just west of the Rockies and less than 100 miles from the Canadian border. Tourism is fast replacing the region's traditional industries of forestry and ranching, with fishing and skiing in Whitefish and the splendors of Glacier National Park nearby. Founded in 1891 with the arrival of the Great Northern Railroad, Kalispell is now a rapidly growing city of more than 14,000.

Travel Season

Summer is the best time to visit this area, which explains the traffic on the roads during July and August. To avoid the crowds, especially around Glacier National Park, plan your trip in June when the weather is starting to warm up, but before tourist season has officially begun. Or to avoid rain, which is very possible in June, come to Kalispell in September. The average high is about 70 degrees then.

Roads & Biking

Back roads in this region fall into two broad categories: recreation and logging. Logging roads are best on the weekend, recreational roads the opposite – and on either, one must watch for wildlife at all times. Montana does have speed limits, but you're allowed 10 mph in leeway to pass another vehicle. Roughly two thirds of Montana's roads are dirt and gravel, and many of these lead to the most scenic spots. Riding a motorcycle capable of accessing these places is recommended.

Maps

○ *The Recreational Map of Western Montana*, GTR Mapping, available at www.gtrmapping.com
○ GM Johnson & Associates, *Montana State Pearl Map* (Laminated) ISBN 1894570669, $6.95

More Information

○ Glacier County www.glaciermt.com
○ Kalispell Chamber of Commerce www.kalispellchamber.com
○ Glacier National Park www.nps.gov/glac

Attractions

❶ Miracle of America Museum (406) 883-6804
❷ Dirty Shame Saloon (406) 295-5439
❸ National Bison Range (406) 644-2211
❹ Flathead Lake
❺ McGinnis Meadows Cattle and Guest Ranch (406) 293-5000
❻ Conrad Mansion (406) 755-2166
❼ Carousel for Missoula (406) 549-8382
❽ Glacier National Park (406) 888-7800

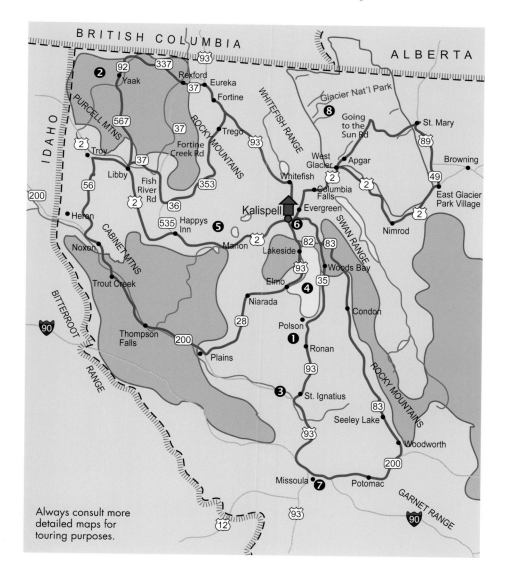

Always consult more detailed maps for touring purposes.

Northeast Oregon
Forgotten Frontier

Text and Photography: Robert Smith

○ *The Painted Hills, near Mitchell, are worth the six-mile detour.*

During my saunter around Northeast Oregon, I realize John Day is a big deal in these parts. There's John Day River, the John Day Fossil Beds and John Day City. Not bad for an ordinary member of John Jacob Astor's 1810 fur trading expedition on its way to establish Astoria, Oregon. Day's distinction? He was stripped of his clothes in an Indian ambush and left to wander naked until rescued…

It's 6:30 p.m., 104 degrees, and I almost envy Day his ignominious disrobement. The Tiger and I steam into John Day City after cresting the 5,100-ft Canyon Creek summit on 395. The valley's brutal heat displaces the cool, cedar-scented air of the Ochoco National Forest. I've just blasted across 150 miles of semi-desert and range from Prineville, shadowing Crooked River and Beaver Creek. The question uppermost in my mind is, where is everyone? It's mid-July: shoals of motor homes suffocate the roads everywhere else, but not in northeast Oregon. It's empty.

My trip began two days earlier in Umatilla, an agricultural industry sprawl on the Columbia River. Rolling west toward Heppner Junction on the straight two-laner in the sweltering heat, I pray for the dawdling trucks ahead to boot it so I can feel some breeze. Even in jeans and a mesh jacket, the afternoon air is stifling. I snap my helmet visor closed: it's actually cooler that way – opening it feels like I'm sticking my head in a pizza oven. Soon I'm cruising south through open farmland to lone where I'm looking for a cut-across to Ruggs. I have to circle back before I find tiny Rhea Creek Road, but it's worth the effort. Wriggling along the creek's side, the pavement is fresh though uneven, and in places dwindles to a single lane.

In Ruggs, my route turns west for Condon, and becomes an archetypal Oregon backroad: long stretches of two-lane chip-seal punctuated with hairpins winding down into a canyon, then twisting up out of the canyon on to more miles of farmland, range and/or semi-desert. Though the twists are intoxicating, I slow my pace after a couple of loose gravel turns and crossing some badly patched potholes. Blithely, the Tiger swoops along, soaking up the ripples through its supple suspension.

Stark bluffs line the country highway from Condon to Fossil, and the Tiger races round the long, fast sweepers. Fossil is my first overnight stop, and I quickly settle on the Bridge Creek Flora Inn, a charming, rustic B&B on the main street. The alternatives are a crusty RV park and a hotel that I never manage to find. I ask owner Lyn Craig where to eat; she points me to the Shamrock Club, which isn't a club and has no apparent Irish connection.

It may sound like a movie cliché, but everyone in the bar really does stop talking, turn and stare as I walk in. I exhale a cheery "Hi", slide onto a stool at the bar and order a Mirror Pond Ale. With normal conversation returning and the glances diminishing, a group of three men and two women walk in. They hesitate, look at me, and then cast eyes around the spare, bare-walled barroom. I realize I'm sitting in "their" place. I pick up my beer and slink off to a corner bench where a painter, brush in one hand, cigarette in the other, is slathering white paint over yards of graffiti. There's a

↻ *Steep bluffs line the John Day River near Kimberly.*

⌒ *Two tons of rust and a ramshackle lodge.*

restaurant behind the bar and I decide to eat there instead…

Next day, after the Bridge Creek Flora's tasty breakfast of eggs and local sausage, I pick up the road to Kimberly. Steep bluffs line the road as it wends along John Day River's North Fork. In Kimberly I search out Hwy 402 to Long Creek and spin across more open range in the relative coolness of the pre-noon. From Long Creek, I head south over Long Creek and Beech Creek summits to Mount Vernon. In the intervening valley, I hit a swarm of locusts splattering my helmet and jacket like a hailstorm, exploding as they do so. Before long, I'm unable to see much through the thick goo on my visor, but thankfully the swarm disperses.

West of Mt. Vernon are two spectacular natural phenomena: Picture Canyon (through which Thomas Condon led a fossil-hunting expedition in 1864, risking a run-in with Union soldiers extracting gold for the Northern cause at nearby Canyon City); and the Painted Hills, where successive layers of volcanic ash have left dark-hued striations in the rolling landscape.

The John Day River cut a deep trough through the rocks at Picture Canyon (more correctly a gorge) between six and fifteen million years ago. Quite why the river chose this path when the surrounding land is almost flat strongly suggests the topography changed over the eons. Just north of the gorge is a vaguely ovine piebald outcrop known as Sheep Rock.

The Painted Hills lie six miles off Highway 26 about 30 miles before Prineville, but are well worth the detour. They remind me of those glass tubes with layers of colored sand sold in trinket-filled tourist shops. The ride into Prineville relieves some of the midday heat as the Tiger and I climb into the Ochoco Mountains. At the forested 4,720-ft Ochoco summit the air is cool, moist and fragrant. I like Prineville. It's a friendly farming town with a prosperous air and a colorful main street.

South is the Prineville Reservoir State Park, a 10-mile detour from the unnumbered Paulina Road. The narrow blacktop twists around the reservoir's north side, ending in a dirt road. The map tells me it's less than five miles to the Paulina Road, so I try out the Tiger's off-highway capa-

↻ *Picture Canyon: famous for fossils – and gold!*

bility. Even grossing around 850lbs, it proves nimble without being too lively, and works best when I let it find its own way through the ruts and rocks.

Rejoining the Paulina Road, it's a mostly straight blast across open range and grassland back to 395 south of Canyon City where gold was discovered in 1861 – the reason Union troops were stationed here, interrupting Thomas Condon's fossil-hunting exploits.

Anyone there?

In the morning, I head south from Prairie City on Summit Prairie Road (County 62, also signed Blue Mountain Hot Springs). It's a purr-fect road for the Tiger – patched and potholed surface with some gravel and the occasional rock, all of which the big cat shrugs off. And, at the 5,899-ft summit, there really is a prairie – wide, open and grassy green – where I turn left onto National Forest Road 16. I'm in the Straw-berry Mountain Wilderness, and wild it is. The narrow track hugs the steep hillside on the 53-mile ride to relative civilization in Unity. Not for the first time I consider what might happen if I went off the road. For the first hour, I see just one car. There's no guarantee anyone would notice a bike at the bottom of a ravine (though the Tiger's Lucifer Orange paint would help), and I could be there indefinitely. If you choose to ride this road alone, make sure someone knows where you are!

Unity is just a gas station/general store, and I head north towards Baker City on Highway 7, featuring a great continuum of long fast sweepers through the Wallowa-Whitman National Forest.

Baker is a delightful city of wide streets, wider sidewalks and grand Victorian build-ings. It was an important stopover on the Oregon Trail, then it burgeoned with the numerous gold discoveries in the region, becoming for a while the most populous city in Oregon. Avoiding the business sprawl

⋂ *The John Day Fossil Beds, Sheep Rock unit, near Dayville.*

⋂ *Local artisans turn juniper twists into unforgettable furniture.*

near I-84, I settle on the clean and com-fortable Bridge Street Inn. The central air-conditioning is a bonus, providing respite from the clanking, wheezing win-dow-mounted boxes everywhere else.

My next destination is the tiny farming town of Ukiah on the other side of the Blue Mountains' Elkhorn Range. I gas up at North Powder and take Anthony Lakes Road west into the mountains. The first five miles it's ugly – ongoing road re-pairs and gravel – followed by a stretch of frost heaves. Then the road breaks

into fresh, smooth tarmac, and I whiz past the struggling cars as the climb gets steeper and more twisted. The 7,400-ft Elkhorn summit is breathtaking, literally, with stunning views across the Thief Valley to the dusky Wallowa Mountains beyond. From the ski village at the summit, the road swoops down towards Ukiah through spooky stands of burnt-out trees, silvery-black against the blue sky.

Ukiah Dan

"I've been here twenty years," says Daniel Vincent, owner of Dan's Ukiah

An Oregonian slice of switchback heaven!

Service, "And they've been trying to get rid of me for fifteen."

Ukiah's two gas stations sit opposite each other on the main street. Dan's gas is 10 cents a gallon cheaper than his rival's, and the station is surrounded by painted signs, mostly decrying government overspending.

"I don't have too much good to say 'bout the guv'ment," says Dan – gruff, brush-haired and walking with the aid of a cane, the result of being shot in the hip during a bank robbery in Alaska, where he owned a million-dollar truck service business.

"Don't see many o' them Limey bikes no more," he says as he tops off the Tiger.

Endless curves under a big blue sky.

The run back to La Grande on 244 sweeps along the Grande Ronde River as it rushes east toward the Snake. I turn north on I-84 for Pendleton, cresting the pretty, thickly forested Blue Mountain summit at 4,100 feet.

Highway 395, south to Nye, climbs into the high plateau. It's harvest time and the lowering sun toasts the fields of fresh-cut grain, rolling golden-brown all the way to the horizon. West towards Heppner on 74, the road deteriorates and the fields fade to barren range as I climb towards the summit. The unstable slope has eroded, leaving broad gaps in the road. A crew is working, but the fix is worse, the road slathered with hot tar and coarse gravel.

On 207, north to Hermiston, I'm fighting the notorious Columbia Gorge wind as it whips across the open grain fields, the hot blast like a fan oven. I cruise into Hermiston, route completed. Just need to find an air-conditioned hotel and a cold beer, with my very own John Day reenactment to follow in privacy…

FACTS AND INFORMATION

Total Mileage

Approximately 936 miles.

In General

This region, featuring many forests, rivers and canyons, is easily accessed by Interstate 84, and is near the Washington and Idaho borders. Perhaps it's the narrow roads, or attractions elsewhere, but the great majority of this particular route in northeast Oregon is almost empty of RVs and tourists, which makes for great motorcycling. Natural beauty abounds – from high plains to the luxuriant green Wallowa Mountains

– in this sportsmen's paradise, and the area is also rich in pioneer history.

Travel Season

Summer can be very hot and the high plateau gets cold in the winter. Shoulder seasons are a good time to visit, in particular April. Of course rain could always be an issue in the spring, so late September is another good time to travel here. There also is less traffic then.

Roads & Biking

Northeast Oregon has many outstanding motorcycling roads, especially

given the general absence of traffic. But much of the area is also remote. If you have to ride alone, make sure you leave route information with a local contact. An unplanned off-road excursion could go undiscovered for days, and cell phone coverage is sparse. The closest motorcycle rental outlet is Road Trip USA in Bend, OR: www.roadtrip-usa.com.

Maps

- The Oregon DOT Official State Map www.odot.state.or.us
- AAA Oregon State Map
- Rand McNally Easy to Read Oregon ISBN 978-0528868566, $4.95

More Information

- Eastern Oregon Visitor's Association www.eova.com
- Oregon Parks & Recreation Dept www.oregonstateparks.org
- Oregon Tourism Information www.traveloregon.com
- Northeast Oregon www.all-oregon.com/regions/northeast.htm

Attractions

❶ Painted Hills
(541) 462-3961
❷ John Day Fossil Beds
(541) 987-2333
❸ National Historic Oregon Trail Interpretive Center
(541) 523-1843
❹ Prineville Reservoir State Park
(800) 551-6949
❺ Pendleton Underground Tours
(800) 226-6398
❻ Lehman Hot Springs
(541) 427-3015
❼ Ritter Hot Springs
(541) 820-3744
❽ Blue Mountain Hot Springs
(541) 820-3744

The West

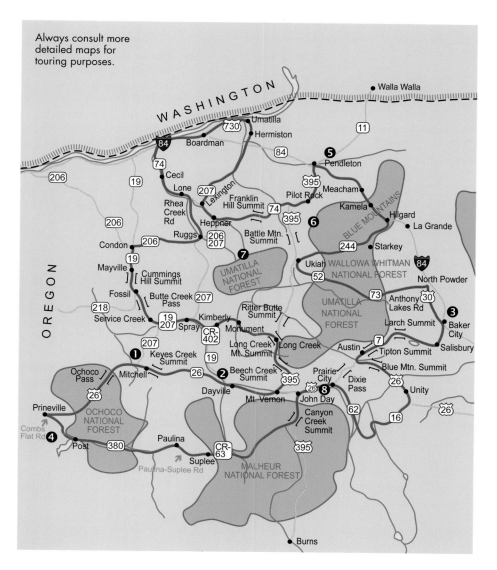

Always consult more detailed maps for touring purposes.

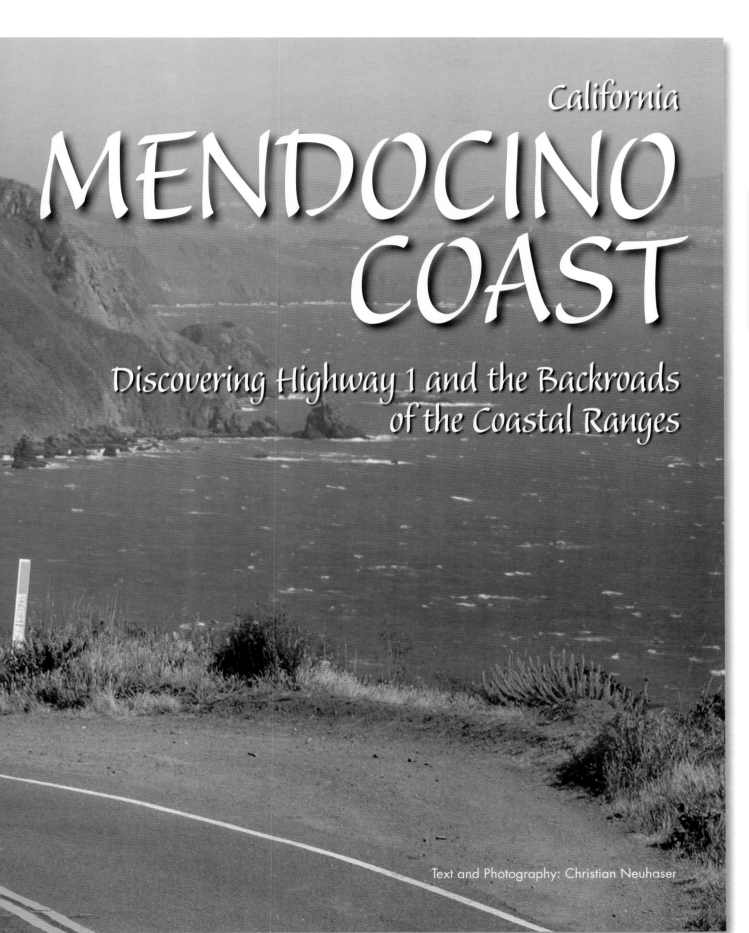

California
MENDOCINO COAST

Discovering Highway 1 and the Backroads of the Coastal Ranges

Text and Photography: Christian Neuhaser

Our excitement is undeniable – accelerating pulses, shallow breathing – as we climb on the plane jetting us to a most beautiful part of California: Highway 1, between San Francisco and Eureka, where the scenic seductions of Marin, Sonoma, Mendocino and Humboldt counties thrill us in the coming days.

◠ *Our tour begins in San Francisco; next up, the Golden Gate Bridge.*

◠ *The cozy village of Miranda welcomes us along the Avenue of the Giants.*
◡ *Fuel stop in downtown of Ferndale.*

The long flight finally over, Christa and I arrive in Los Angeles to collect our motorcycles, an Interceptor and a Honda 919. Luggage firmly affixed, we hit the road to San Francisco.

Our breakfast the next day in Ghiradelli Square is composed of tasty bagels, steaming coffee (from the renowned Boudin Bakery), and the breathtaking view across the waters that extend from Fisherman's Wharf. Alcatraz, "The Rock," and its phantoms are still out there, surrounded by the blue-green sea. Bright white sails dip and scurry, tacking against the azure sky.

It all certainly sets the mood for an adventurous escape as we ride over the Golden Gate Bridge past Sausalito (on Hwy 1), and turning left toward Muir Beach. The highway begins to snake there, between the Golden Gate National Recreation Area and Mount Tamalpais State Park. My Interceptor handles well through the wide sweepers and tight turns, and so does the 919, from what I can tell in the mirror. Suddenly, after about 18 miles, the first grand view of the ocean opens out before us. The thought of riding along without a stop to soak in this sight is an incomprehensible notion. A turnout appears as if on cue along the rough coastline. The water wildly thrashes the rocks, launching spumes of spray that sparkle far below the coastal road. Engines stilled, we pull our helmets off and turn our noses into the whipping, saline breeze.

"It's cold today," Christa says. "But this overlook certainly warms the heart and soul – isn't that great?" I add, extending an arm to pan the whole horizon.

Looking down to my left, I spy our veering route on Hwy 1. I didn't expect in my boldest dreams such an incredible course along the shoreline. Its pattern looks like an old-time roller coaster. Up, down, left, right, and wide and tight – providing everything a biker wishes for to stir the blood.

Somewhere along this asphalt gauntlet, I check our saddlebags – still there, fitting snugly on our bikes – and then we open up our throttles again and head for Bodega Bay and lunch. With big smiles and shining eyes we sweep up and over, down, around, and through this fantastic combination of curves.

"What would you like to drink?" our waitress asks, trying to pull us from our dreams.

"Fish and chips," I answer idly, still rolling into corners. "Oh, sorry, I mean iced tea *and* fish and chips."

"It's okay, Huh-n. You're not the only one who's still on the road when sitting down here."

I perked up then. "You're from North Carolina, aren't you?" I ask.

"And what gave it away, Huh-n?"

"It's the huh-n, hon," I quip to general mirth.

If the name Bodega prompts some dim, spooky memory, you're right. Five miles east of here, one finds much of the scenery filmed in Hitchcock's classic, *The Birds*. But we decide to frolic on our bikes without the creep-out factor and, instead, swing the Hondas through the curves of Hwy 1, enjoying the overwhelming visions at each of the different bays and the unbelievable variety of colors in the wildflowers passed along the way.

Arts and Coffee

The light is great and the opportunity unsurpassed for taking pictures. But it's hard to find just the right spot because there are simply too many new impressions to catalogue behind every curve. And so, to cover the next 58 miles we need almost three hours. And then came another pleasant discovery, Gualala, a cozy little village by the sea. This charming place invites you to stop and rest a spell, to frequent its bewitching restaurants, the small, artsy stores, and a nice café where cappuccinos and tasty coconut cookies appease our empty stomachs. To start up again in such a relaxing atmosphere is difficult,

↻ *We leave The Redwood Haus filled with Angelika's great food and Oluf's unbelievable motorcycle stories.*

↻ *Cornering on the way to Point Reyes.*

● *Mendocino gleams in the morning sun.*

but our next target is only 60 miles away. The road is smoother and our ride proceeds briskly.

Mendocino, the next highlight, was founded in the 18th century but achieved its current notoriety in the 1960s as an artists' colony. Now a very upscale tourist magnet, it still promotes the creative flair. Unfortunately for the photographer in me, it's too late for shooting and check-in time at Fort Bragg SM8 is drawing nigh. Ten miles onward, we end a speedy ride and find the comforts of a bed.

Giants Among Us

Great swathes of morning mist threaten to hug the coast. But bad conditions can't stop us from satisfying our curiosity about the next 123 miles.

The first 16 miles to Westport are smooth rolling and just the right warm-up for tires, bike, and rider. In my case, I'm *too* awake after only the first mile because my leather jacket, great for warmer climates, isn't right for 45 degrees and I have to pull off in West-

port to layer better with a thick long-sleeved shirt. This amuses Christa – My husband, the wimp.

"Easy for you to talk, sitting there in your lined jacket."

"I do feel incredibly *warm* and *cozy*," she taunts, hugging herself.

The next few miles to Leggett are perfect: racetrack grip, wide and tight turns, and lots of giddy hilliness. And the chilling fog is gone. The blue sky shines like porcelain above the forest as I snake the Interceptor around massive redwoods. If the guy who built this road didn't have a soft spot for motorcyclists, it doesn't show. Encountering little traffic and comfortable at last, I put on more and more speed; Christa follows easily, circling her 919 through the curves with elegance. She's smiling.

The roaring madness ends after 27 miles when we arrive in Leggett. I'm hot in two different ways. I crave more of these roads and no longer need my thick 49ers sweatshirt. We see the signs directing us to the Redwood National Park and enter, passing through the arch carved in the

trunk of another gargantuan tree. We hit 101 towards Phillipsville and turn onto a route running 24 miles through deep, dark, mystical, woods – the Avenue of the Giants. Very few sunrays break through the dense branches, and at times this primeval surround is so impressive I forget to breathe. These noble, ancient trees, some 2,000 years old, are the tallest in the world, growing to heights of 360 feet; and no matter its size, any ambulatory being with half a brain has to feel dwarfed here.

Reaching Pepperwood, taking 101 again for 19 miles, we roll upon the town of Fortuna and happily allow the staff of the local microbrewery, The Eel River Brewing Company, to spoil us with great food, service, and a number of tasty draughts.

Heading West

"Where are we off to today?" Christa chirps the next morning.

"We cruise west, my dear," I answer in kind, with a forecast of clear skies beckoning although bone-chilling temperatures persist this early in the day.

First up: Ferndale, an old Victorian town. The enchanting homes and manicured lawns lining the way through town inspire us to slow to a jogging clip and take it all in. Following the signs to Petrolia places us on a very steep and narrow road with all sorts of bumps and loose gravel creating challenges that we tackle in slow motion. Then a wonderful ride over lush green hills and through narrow valleys exceeds all expectations. A last steep hill before a grand and glorious view rivets our attention at the overlook to Cape Mendocino, the most westerly point in the contiguous states. We stop for a moment, open the visors, and gulp the salted air.

Petrolia, Honeydew, Ettersburg, and Briceland are small villages passed on the way to Redway. The ride through the Rainbow Ridge and the King Mountain Range is about 75 miles, so be sure to have enough petrol in the tank. We stop for coffee and lunch in a really nice town, Garberville, mainly cited as a tourist stop that boasts a range of outdoor pursuits in the Six Rivers National Forest.

For those with time to hang out and observe the bustle in the street, one of Garberville's sidewalk cafés fills the bill to a tee. But we have to focus on our target, Fort Bragg. Highway 101 to Wilitis is a relaxing ride and, after these Lost Coast experiences, it's the way to warm up for Hwy 20.

The last 35 miles of roadway is the kind of stretch I never want to end. I open the throttle to sweep through the curves, and immediately we find the rhythm. Great asphalt and minimal traffic invite us to hurtle along at breathtaking speed; and Christa, up to the task, sticks like glue to my rear tire all the way to Fort Bragg. Captain's Log: 190 miles on surfaces ranging from smooth, sweet curves to loose gravel, and bone-jarring bumps and holes – an exhilarating ride.

Another Day in Paradise

Fort Bragg to Santa Rosa is the day's plan. We aren't in much of a hurry today and sleep in a little longer than normal, which also allows us to start out without contending with the dangers of view-obscuring fog. We take Hwy 1 south to Albion. In Albion we take a left toward Boonville. Highway 128 is a smooth ride through dense woods, and after 27 miles, we hang a right on Mountain View Road. These 30 miles snaking over the Coastal Range are more than enough to enliven any biker's spirits. Very little traffic and great road conditions enhance the experience, but leaning left to right in fast-change series is a lot of work and we welcome the rest the fresh sea breeze signals. Once more, we stop in Gualala for coffee and find out, during a nice chat with an Officer Ryan, that the way to Annapolis offers an entertaining ride to Santa Rosa. Thanking him for the tip, we start our Hondas for the next round.

➲ *The narrow, bump-riddled road to Cape Mendocino, the westernmost point in California.*

The ensuing miles aren't much of a secret for local motorcyclists. We ran across crotch rockets, naked bikes, enduros, and even members of the Harley crowd. Nice scenery: You choose a leader and follow. Safely, but at a fairly rapid clip, flying through the curves, we add some sparking scratches to the asphalt. It's a very cool ride! Pausing at the turnout for the Sonoma Lake overlook, I reach for a smoke and wait for Christa. But just when I flick my lighter open, she sweeps around the curve, ignores me, and barrels on. I jump aboard, close my visor, and scat to catch her. Two miles on, she's looking in the mirror, waving – thumb's up.

Still traveling 128, past the incredibly picturesque hills of vineyard country, we ride towards Santa Rosa. Unloading our bikes, I turn to Christa. "Ho-hum. Just another day in paradise," I say. "What do *you* think?" Christa readily agrees, and we end our wonderful day wandering Santa Rosa's historic district and settling in to chow down at an Italian restaurant.

A Short Day

Filled with great restaurants, Fourth Street in Santa Rosa lures us back for a wonderful breakfast at The Omelette Express. We certainly do need it before taking on 116, better known as the Russian River Valley. The 36-mile ride to the coast is not only another gorgeous outing – it has to rank well up on the list of "Best Ways to the Coast," presenting a smooth, snaking tour along the river toward Jenner. Suffice it to say, we're more than a little disheartened when it's over and have to turn left on Hwy 1.

In Point Reyes Station, we stop for lunch at The Station House Cafe. Great food spoils us again and a short nap after would be the logical choice. But we have other plans: Point Reyes National Seashore. The way to the lighthouse ushers in a different world. Rolling hills and a wide-open view closely resemble a Scottish landscape, a feeling

↻ Pale morning panorama: Coastal beauty, rising fog.

supported by the rough gusting winds. Farms and cattle adorn the landscape, and the 15-minute walk to the lighthouse is strenuous enough to shed some of the delicious, caloric indulgence we've put on the last couple of days.

Early in the afternoon we arrive in Stinson Beach and I can't help stopping when spotting "Zimmer mit Frühstück" (Bed & Breakfast) on the sign at The Redwoods Haus. A touch of home. *Maybe they speak German?* It turns out they don't. Oluf and Angelika are Americans with a great sense of humor. They advertise their B&B in another language, which

makes sense as a way of widening the net and all that. And now that we're here, we relax and enjoy the wild stories Oluf tells, the good breakfast Angelika prepares, and all the cozy comforts of the place.

The next morning we carve our way along the Marin Headlands toward San Francisco and stop at the fabulous Point Bonita, which presents a last chance to fully luxuriate in the rugged magnificence of the sea-swept panorama. Our tour is ending, but our return home is freighted with so many vibrant memories we'll never truly leave this stretch of coastal California. 🏍

↻ Dwarfed by botanical behemoths: The Avenue of the Giants.

Total Mileage

Approximately 778 miles.

In General

The whole area offers endless possibilities for an unforgettable motorcycle vacation. Highway 1 N is the route to follow when touring Marin, Sonoma, Mendocino, and Humboldt counties. This popular road leads from San Francisco to Leggett, where it runs into 101. Offering great sightseeing and a stunning variety of landscapes – rocky coastline, golden hills, and gigantic redwood trees.

The second part of the tour is an underestimated route between the Sacramento Valley and the coast. This road snakes through the coastal ranges and throws out many challenging curves with a lot of grip and little traffic.

Travel Season

Northern California is a great place for rides between mid-April to mid-November although it still can be pretty cool then, especially along the coast; so consider packing long johns. The valleys can be very hot and within a mere 25 miles there's often a difference in temperature of 30°F.

Roads & Biking

Hwy 1 is a great road for twists and turns, and its asphalt condition is most inviting for aggressive riding. But be careful: some turns are covered with loose gravel and bigger stones. Wind gusts and fog also can pose problems. The roads between the Sacramento Valley and the coast, crossing the coastal ranges, present challenges for every motorcyclist – narrow and winding with bumps on the best line at times that deserve your full attention. The road between Honeydew, Ettersburg, and Redway is paved even though your map may indicate otherwise.

Maps

- *California State Map*
  Rand McNally & Company
  0528995014, $4.95
- *American Map*
  Road Atlas 2009 Standard
  0841628432, $14.95

More Information

- Mendocino Coast & County Travel Directory
  www.mendocino.org
- Sonoma County Wine Country
  www.sonoma.com
- California State Parks
  www.parks.ca.gov

Attractions

❶ Fisherman's Wharf
❷ Safari West Wildlife Preserve and African Tent Camp
  (707) 579-2551
❸ The Carson Mansion
  (707) 445-8775
❹ Drive Thru Tree Park
  (707) 925-6363
❺ Russian Gulch State Park
  (707) 937-5804
❻ Avenue of the Giants
❼ Point Reyes Lighthouse
  (415) 669-1534
❽ Robert Hunter Winery
  (707) 328-0173

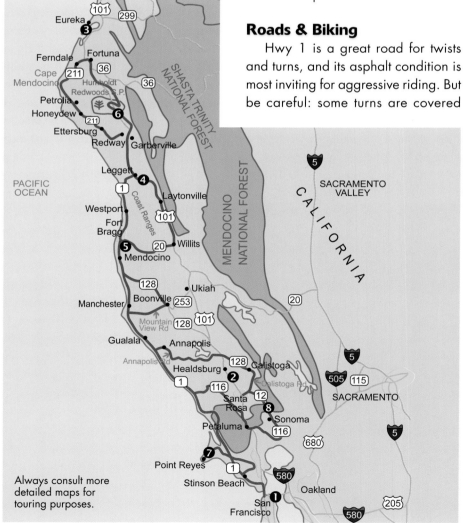

Always consult more detailed maps for touring purposes.

Tour Planning Nuts & Bolts

Where to go and what kind of tour you'd like to take are the two most important decisions you'll make. Everything else pretty much follows.

What kind of tour?

1. Road trip or sightseeing? Most often, a tour will be a mixture of riding for the fun of it and visiting interesting places.
2. Destination or journey? Is where you're going more important than how you get there?
3. Solo or group?
4. Where, when and how long? If you already know where you want to go, when's the best time to go, and how much time should you allow?
5. Camping or motels? Or a mixture?

Route planning

So, now you know roughly where you're going and when. How do you decide what roads to take? First, estimate your daily mileage. A comfortable pace is maybe 200 miles a day, which gives time to linger over lunch and stop to smell the roses; plan for 300 or more if you're prepared to put in the hours. When you're making time on the Interstate, it's not difficult to average 50 mph, including gas and coffee stops, and 400 miles a day becomes feasible. But don't try to travel too far: Fatigue can be lethal.

Applying these guidelines should give you a rough idea of the distance you can travel in the time you have. Next, prioritize the places you want to see and the roads you want to travel.

For destinations and sightseeing, federal, state and local guides are always helpful. Any reliable search engine will turn up what you need. I always look for any Scenic Byways in the region I'm visiting at www.byways.org.

For great riding roads, try Destination Highways, www.destinationhighways.com (Washington, Oregon and Northern California), Mad Maps, www.madmaps.com (California), www.motorcycleadventuremaps.com (Blue Ridge & Smoky Mountains), www.motorcycleroads.us (national), and www.pashnit.com (California again).

Two further considerations: weather and traffic. Obvious no-nos would be Yellowstone or Yosemite Park in August (traffic) and much of the Rockies in April (snow). Online weather guides like www.weather.com are invaluable, and you can get historical climate information from www.worldclimate.com. *The Times Books World Weather Guide* by E. A. Pearce, ASIN 0812918819 is a useful reference.

For detailed planning, you'll need maps. AAA and Rand McNally are a good start, but get a detailed local map, too. I've often found that roads marked paved on one map are shown unpaved on another. Don't rely solely on GPS maps: always have paper backups.

Leave a couple of days free in your schedule. Serendipity is one of the charms of motorcycle touring, and some slack will allow you time to linger in a special place.

Equipment planning

I have a checklist I refer to before every tour. I don't always take everything on the list, but it ensures I haven't forgotten anything important. Though you'll want to make your own list, mine includes these items: multi-tool, cell phone, maps, flashlight, camera, film, batteries, sunscreen, notebook, pens, rain gear, first-aid kit, puncture kit, disc lock, cash, etc.

Make sure your bike is primed for the length of the trip. Tires? Oil changes? Chain? Scheduled maintenance? Verify that your AAA membership is up to date, too, and that enough funds are available in your credit card account for emergency repairs.

When packing for a trip, take half the clothes and twice the money! Simplistic, perhaps, but most of us do pack too much. *Cycle World's* Peter Egan famously travels with his oldest underwear so he can simply trash it along the way.

Make sure your riding gear will survive the trip. There's a big difference between getting caught in a shower riding to the coffee bar and spending all day plowing through a rainstorm. At 60 mph with a still air temperature of 50 degrees, the wind chill factor is 25 degrees. Do the math! If wet, evaporation will reduce body temperature even more. Motorcycling and hypothermia don't mix! When in doubt, buy new gear and test it well before you go; and perhaps you'll need to add a heated vest, too.

Contingency planning

Plan for the worst, and it will probably never happen - a travel first-aid kit is a must. Whenever you're roaming alone, make sure someone has a copy of your route and approximate schedule. Traveling outside of North America brings on a whole new set of factors, such as passports and visas; disease prevention; emergency preparedness; carnets de passage, etc. Contemplating such an undertaking requires specific preparations beyond the scope of this article.

Happy trails!

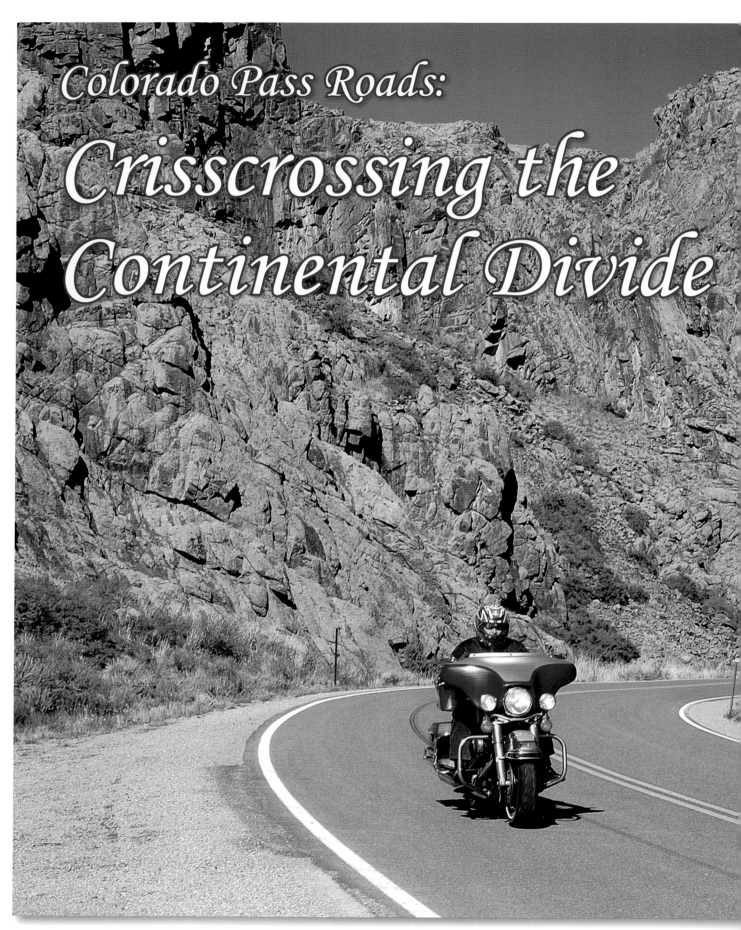

Colorado Pass Roads:
Crisscrossing the Continental Divide

Parked at Extended Stay America in the Denver suburb of Aurora, I make sure the reinforced steel cable lock wraps a round the front wheel and frame of my '04 Electra Glide. This baby's goin' nowhere. The next morning I'm packed, ready to roll, and slide the key into the barrel. It jams solid. I guess I was right. We're not going anywhere...

Text and Photography: Robert Smith

○ *South Park City, a recreated 1880's mining town near Hoosier Pass.*

○ *Fall colors dapple the aspens near Independence Pass.*

☉ *Hwy 6: Above the tree line on the way to Loveland Pass.*

AAA responds to my panic call, but when the errant key shears off, it's locksmith time. An hour later, Jesus from Foothills Lock and Key slices through the cable with an angle grinder. Emergency over, and I'm finally on my way.

Four days, 12 passes

I turn off Interstate 70 west of Denver for Lookout Mountain. The Glide and I wind to the summit on gloriously curvy tarmac lined with fields and shade trees. William Cody was visiting his sister Louisa in Denver in December 1916 when his health failed. He died there shortly after. Louisa buried him on Lookout Mountain, a move disputed by Cody, Wyoming, the town Buffalo Bill founded. The dispute was formally resolved with a ceremonial burying of hatchets…in 1997!

Back on 70, I'm cruising past Idaho Springs when a sign advertising "Tommyknocker Pub and Brewery" catches my eye. In mining lore, Tommyknockers were mischievous elves who blew out lamps or hid shovels, but they also revealed the richest veins. The side streets of this former mining town hide rows of refurbished miner cottages, and the grand frontage lining Miner Street reflect an earlier affluence. I have to pass on the brewpub. There's riding to do.

Berthoud Pass: 11,315 ft.

Stalled in construction on Highway 40 toward Granby, I buy water and peanuts at the Last General Store, the peanut bag blown up like a balloon in the thin air. Hwy 40 winds over the Berthoud Pass's turns, a heady mix of sweepers, hairpins and gentle bends, as I blast past grinding semi-trucks to the summit.

Over the pass, I descend steadily into Granby through manufactured ski resorts. The weather is closing in, and rain is falling in the surrounding mountains. I turn east for Kremmling, following the Colorado River as it pours through steep-sided Byers Canyon. That this rushing stream could be the source of a mighty waterway irrigating California is awe-inspiring.

Fremont Pass: 11,318 ft.

In Kremmling I ask the gas jockey if it'll rain. "Ninety-five percent certain," she says. I get into my rain gear. Five miles later on Highway 9, I'm stuck in another construction holdup when the precipitation starts. A blustery chill buffets the Glide and the temperature plummets as I roll back toward Copper Mountain on I-70. While I'm climbing Highway 9's winding two-laner toward Fremont Pass, the drizzle threatens sleet, yet miraculous shafts of crimson sunlight split the clouds. Leaving the precipitation at the pass, I roll into Leadville under asphalt-colored clouds.

Tennessee Pass: 10,424 ft.

At 10,200 feet, Leadville, a charming ex-mining town of un-restored buildings, is one of Colorado's highest communities. It's refreshingly free of tourist kitsch, too – except for the 1879 saloon, now an Irish pub, with its retro-western style boardwalk and hitching posts.

One more pass today, and it's a marvel, though barely higher than Leadville itself. Highway 24 switchbacks along the sheer wall of a towering cliff and over ravine-leaping bridges that seem to defy civil engineering principles.

I rejoin I-70 west for the drag into Glenwood Springs, and there's another treat in store: Glenwood Canyon. A natural miracle, the walls of purple-grey rock are laminated like a layer cake, and with the clouds now behind me, the cake's striations glow crimson in the setting sun. But the Colorado DOT

didn't account for this phenomenon and provide any photo-op pullouts...

In the gathering dusk, I check into the comfortable Silver Spruce Inn. My room is spacious, squeaky clean, with a full kitchen, and very reasonably priced, considering my proximity to Vail and Aspen.

Independence Pass 12,093 ft.

I can't help noticing how so many Colorado cities are named for their prosaic past activities: Leadville, Gypsum, Granite, Basalt, Carbondale. Eighty-two carries me through the last two, now primarily resort service towns, on the gradual climb from Glenwood's 5,600 feet to Aspen's 7,900. The famous resort's downtown is packed with tony stores and chic cafes, and the swank houses on the surrounding streets compete for the glorious views with huge picture windows and Alpine façades.

↻ *Fresh mountain air and cool, clear water! Twin Lakes.*

○ *An amazing view of Colorado's impressive landscape.*

rocky terrain is scarred and scraped. The last push to the pass is steep and the Glide gasps for air. Fifth gear is unusable, and fourth is a struggle. The howling wind over the exposed pass is bitter, but the sun is hot, and unlike the previous day there's not a cloud in the sky.

Monarch Pass: 11,312 ft.

Leaving the Aspen sightseers behind, I'm winding through tunnels of trees trying on their fall colors. Not bright reds and oranges like eastern maples, but a vivid yellow-rust contrasting with the dark evergreens. Then a broad valley opens between the magnificent blue Twin Lakes. I'm in high-country range and farmland under an almost indigo sky. Through Buena Vista, true to its name, the basin is now lined with snow-capped 14,000-foot peaks; then on to Salida, once a prosperous railroad junction town, but now an "historic" tourist destination.

A wonderful riding road south from Aspen, Highway 82 is narrow and winding, following the rock face as it deeks in and out, before opening into a wider two-lane with long sweepers and hairpins. I'm above the tree line now and the barren,

↻ *The Glide's unhurried pace allows time for scenic appreciation.*

I join broad, busy 50 west toward Gunnison, with fast sweepers up to Monarch Pass and its magnificent views. Descending west from the pass is frustrating: motor homes clog the only downhill lane, and passing is verboten.

North Cochetopa Pass: 10,149 ft.

Just before Gunnison, I turn southeast across open range on 114. The pass is undramatic with a barely noticeable climb, and just a few wide, sweeping bends near the top. South from Saguache, 285 heads arrow-straight across board-flat potato fields, and I idly count down the crossroads to Monte Vista: 25-mile Road, 24-mile Road...

The tidy, friendly town's 1930's hotel, Budget Host Monte Villa Inn, offers quaint rooms with traditional furniture: a refreshing change from soulless modern motels.

La Veta Pass: 9,413 ft.

East from Alamosa on 160, I'm skirting the Sangre de Cristo Mountains, and the climb to the pass is gentle and fast. From Walsenburg, the Glide stretches its legs on I-25 as far as Colorado City, turning on 196 for Silver City. The climb is steady and the road winds gently into the mountains through the San Isabel Forest. The trees start as ponderosa pines, but the aspens increase steadily until they dominate. I crest another pass, the Beulah Divide, but it would "pass" unnoticed but for the sign.

I see signs for Bishop's Castle, the name of an English border town. Instead, a "real" castle appears through the trees, with a gothic stone turret and a wrought iron dragon's head. For over 40 years, Jim Bishop has been building this fantastic structure that started as a family cabin in the woods. Now its buttresses and towers peer over the surrounding forest. I clamber up the steep iron staircase to explore, but the open ironwork walkways and bridges trigger my vertigo. Mr. Bishop has allotted scant consideration to the subject of guardrails in his soaring designs.

Wilkerson Pass: 9,502 ft.

Highway 69 takes me north to Texas Creek, mostly in open range and sometimes following the old Denver & Rio Grande railroad. Then come the splendid curves of 50 as it winds east between tall bluffs along the Arkansas River. By the turnoff to Hartsel, a sign for Royal Gorge initiates a detour. There's a full "theme park" with suspension bridge, airtram rides and a "skycoaster," but I can also see the gorge from the parking lot. Hundreds of feet below, the Arkansas River crashes through a narrow canyon less than 50 feet wide. Impressive.

North to Hartsel over more rolling range, and 11 Mile State Park provides delightful twists through the aspens. I turn east on 24 for the short climb to Wilkerson Pass: this is already high country and the pass is barely noticeable but for some climbing turns and ragged cliffs. Heavily trafficked, 24 sweeps gently over more range into Woodland Park, elevation 8,437 ft.

Kenosha Pass: 10,001 ft. and Red Hill Pass: 9,986 ft.

Heading north on 67 for Deckers, I'm running through stands of ponderosa pine on what must be a weekend commuter road to the lakes and woodlands in the surrounding hills. I'm charmed by Jacob's Creek, a delightful one-church, one rusty gas pump town. Roads are good, too, with lots of twisties as we spin through canyons and creek-side valleys. I'm surprised not to find more Friday evacuees riding the roads, motorcycles are few and far between, but truck traffic on 285 West is thick as I spin up through the aspens to the sweeping pass.

♫ *North Cochetopa Pass: a shallow climb and wide, sweeping bends.*

♯ *Looking for something liquid in legendary Leadville.*

Highway 50 winds alongside the Arkansas River.

Kenosha opens onto the vast San Luis Valley before the gentle push to Red Hill Pass, a shallow rise with sweeping bends. Fairplay is home to South Park City, a reproduction 1880's mining boomtown with actors in period costume.

Hoosier Pass: 11,539 ft.

Highway 9 starts a steady climb north before the main push to Hoosier Pass. The road skirts the valley's east side with 14,000-foot Mt. Lincoln to the west. Some bends lurk near the pass, but it's mainly a straight run. The views are magnificent. We're above the tree line, and the bald peaks, softer and rounder than the Canadian Rockies, reflect scatterings of glacial ice. A manufactured ski town, all steel roofs, stucco and picture windows, Breckenridge appears to be the working ski bum's answer to more traditional Aspen.

Loveland Pass: 11,990 ft.

From Dillon, Highway 6's four-lanes climb toward the Keystone ski resort, narrowing to two lanes for the long sweeping climb to the pass. Devoid of trees, the scenery is starkly magnificent, and the curves lay exposed to view for miles. I linger at the pass, watching trucks grow from tiny dots thousands of feet below to become the growling, grinding monsters that rumble past me. Interstate 70, a distant stripe across the valley below, beckons me back to Denver.

But of course there's much more to Colorado than high passes. I'll be back.

Historic farmhouses await restoration near Parkdale.

66

Colorado
FACTS AND INFORMATION

Total Mileage

Approximately 1,008 miles.

In General

Colorado's pass roads are some of the highest in the country, climbing to more than 12,000 feet, so weather is an important consideration. It can snow any time of the year at these altitudes. Check the forecast carefully. And if your bike is carbureted (rather than fuel injected), you might need a change of jetting. The reward: riding above the tree line in the crisp air under azure skies on superb mountain roads. Don't forget your sunscreen!

Travel Season

In this area, weather often varies throughout the course of a day's ride. With this in mind, it's best to come prepared with a multi-climate jacket and rain gear. As one rides through the passes, the temperature will gradually turn cooler as the elevation rises. For this reason, the riding season in Colorado begins late in the year. June and July are ideal months to travel here. At the very earliest, come in May.

Roads & Biking

Colorado's DOT does a great job of maintenance: most roads are evenly surfaced and in good repair. However, this does mean construction delays in summer; but that's a small price to pay. Watch out for big rigs on the major passes. Truckers seem to prefer the passes to the Interstate.

Maps

- *Colorado Road & Recreation Atlas*
  Benchmark Maps
  ISBN 0929591941, $24.95
- *Rand McNally Colorado:*
  Easyfinder; Highways & Interstates

Rand McNally and Company
ISBN 0528856197, $7.95

More Information

- Colorado Tourism Office
  www.colorado.com
- Glenwood Springs Chamber of Commerce
  www.visitglenwood.com
- Colorado State Parks
  www.parks.state.co.us
- A Guide to Historic & Scenic Leadville & Twin Lakes, Colorado
  www.leadville.com

Attractions

❶ Buffalo Bill Museum & Grave
(303) 526-0744
❷ Vapor Caves & Yampah Spa
(970) 945-0667
❸ Silver Queen Gondola on Aspen Mountain
(970) 923-1227
❹ Bishop Castle
❺ Rocky Mountain Dinosaur Resource Center
(719) 686-1820
❻ South Park City
(719) 836-2387

The West

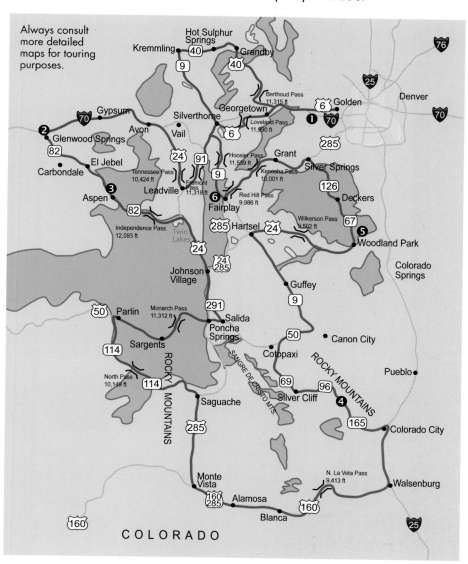

Always consult more detailed maps for touring purposes.

The Southwest

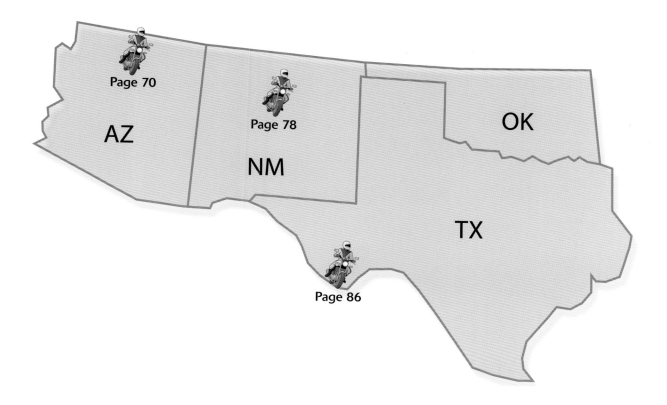

Page 70

AZ

Page 78

NM

OK

TX

Page 86

The southwestern states comprise a truly enchanting landscape. From the big blue sky and rolling plains of Oklahoma and Texas to the canyon pueblos of ancient Native American civilizations in New Mexico and Arizona, the Southwest offers an expansive canvas of fascinating destinations to explore.

Venturing south to the Big Bend Country along the Rio Grande River, travelers discover that there really are mountains in Texas, rising above the arid landscape. A few hundred miles north is the Texas Hill Country, made famous by country-singing legends and beguiling byways.

Santa Fe, New Mexico, a former Spanish colonial outpost, is both the oldest state capital in America and a gentrified arts colony replete with handsome adobe architecture. Exploring further west reveals two iconic geographic features of the Southwest: the haunting mesas of Monument Valley and a canyon so stupendously large and deep that it was named the 'Grand' Canyon. So, mount up partner – we're headed to the Southwest.

Northern Arizona
Grand Canyon Country

I awake in Flagstaff to a dusting of snow on the trees and bushes. More of the same is heaped upon the naked rock that crowns Humphrey's Peak, the highest point in Arizona. This sharp summit, stretching 12,633 feet above this old railroad town, tears holes in the fast-moving storm clouds, and I'll come to use it like the North Star to navigate in Northern Arizona.

Text and Photography: Troy Hendrick

The bird's eye view from the pinnacle takes in the Mogollon Rim to the southeast, the Hopi and Navajo Nations to the east and north, and the Grand Canyon to the north. I know the ride to these destinations rolls through some of the world's most famous scenery – and to top it off, I'm lucky enough to be trying out the Gold Wing 1800.

Flagstaff

For the time being, though, I've spent two days holed up in Flagstaff, waiting out a late-April snowstorm that has kept the streets covered. I arrived the day before from Phoenix, where it was 85 degrees. The Arizona weather this time of year can be so fickle from one hour and one elevation to the next that snapping the liner in and out of my jacket becomes as common as a gas refill. From the look of things, a chilly wind blowing and dark clouds forming above, I'll have to bide my time at least one more day.

On the other hand, Flagstaff is not such a bad place to be sidelined. The city stretches right up to the feet of the San Francisco Peaks, and Humphrey's Peak is a postcard backdrop for the town of artists, students, and outdoor adventurers. Grateful Dead stickers adorn decayed station wagons and shiny SUVs alike. Dreadlocks are as ubiquitous as fleece jackets here, and I even heard one guy refer to the town as "The *Flag*, man."

Flagstaff offers plenty to see and do. The city's historic district, with its breweries, art galleries, and Native American jewelry stores is a bustling, vibrant place. The heavy rumbling of trains frequently passing alongside Route 66 and right through downtown provides a distinct aural pulse. There are also the attractions of several museums, including the Museum of Northern Arizona (on the way to the Grand Canyon along US 180), an observatory, and three national monuments within easy driving distance. The famous Red Rocks and Sedona are located just a twisty, half-hour drive south of Flagstaff into the Oak Creek Canyon.

Finally on the Road to the Grand Canyon

The next morning is chilly, but the sun is shining and the snow has melted from the roads. The anticipation almost over, the Grand Canyon soon in sight, I snap the liner into my riding jacket and point the

↻ *Lonesome, looking for company – even a rattlesnake would be nice.*

Wing north out of Flagstaff. Past Humphrey's Peak on my right, and letting the rpm climb high, I'm ascending into the Kaibab National Forest. When the road begins to flatten out, I'm on top of the Coconino Plateau, part of the larger Colorado Plateau.

A few sweepers through the northern stretches of the San Francisco Peaks give way to the long and predominantly straight US 180. Pinyon pine forests stretch to the edge of the horizon along most of the plateau, but Humphrey's Peak is always visible in the rearview mirror. The rising sun begins to warm the air, and my excitement about seeing the greatest natural wonder in North America grows stronger.

Most visitors first see the Canyon, invisible on the approach, when they leave their vehicles and carefully step to the edge of the great divide. Eighteen miles away is the opposite edge of the great chasm, like another world altogether, and such is the drama of the sight that it's nearly inconceivable that both worlds could be connected. But on the canyon floor, a mile down, the serpentine blue-green ribbon that has carved this mammoth gorge from the earth's crust joins these worlds again. It's taken the Colorado River several million years of rock gouging to produce this stunning landscape. Looking from the canyon's edge it seems the view is limitless – sometimes it can be around 50 miles – and there is nothing in sight to suggest the canyon ends.

Many tourists initially experience the Grand Canyon from Mather Point, and further west along the South Rim, Yavapai Point is the next stop for a vertiginous view. From there, the road winds down to Grand Canyon Village, where the free shuttle bus service carries visitors from viewpoint to viewpoint the next eight miles west to Hermit Point. Without auto accessibility, this area is the least crowded and offers the most breathtaking views.

♦ *Cruising in the endless expanse of Northern Arizona.*

Heading east out of the park, I cruise down Desert Drive. The 25-mile stretch has several viewpoints of the southern and eastern edges of the Canyon, and a few nicely linked curves. I don't get to lean as much as I'd like given the number of reasonable RVers taking their time. This nice slow pace predominates around the Canyon during the off-season. In the heart of summer, however, these routes can be as congested as the rush-hour thoroughfares in any major city.

About 70 million years ago, a large mass of what is now the southwestern United States began rising due to tectonic pressures. Starting close to sea level, the Colorado Plateau uplifted over 10,000 feet, and the Canyon's formation began five to six million years ago as water drained from the western Rocky Mountains. The water carried silt, gravel, and rocks on its journey to the Gulf of California. This loose aggregate made a very effective saw to cut into the arid landscape around Grand Canyon National Park. A geological and chronological cross-section of the American southwest, the canyon walls are composed of at least 12 distinct layers of rock, the oldest of which is 1.8 billion years old. The end result of these ancient forces – the Grand Canyon – is 277 miles long, a mile deep, and up to eighteen miles wide.

The trip out of the Canyon on SR 64 foreshadows the scenery encountered over the next two days in my ride through the sacred lands of the Southwestern tribes. A great plateau rises above the road on the right, with ochre and rust-colored earth exposed. Here, where the Colorado Plateau has nearly completed its drastic transition from the desert flatlands to the south, the wind frequently howls. Dirt devils twirl hypnotically, skipping along the orange landscape. The Little Colorado River, flowing parallel to SR 64 on the left, has carved it's own cleft in the landscape – not so dramatic, but impressive nonetheless.

From the road, Navajo vendors displaying their wares under cloth shelters are the only indication of man's presence in this sprawling expanse. A sucker for silver and turquoise, I can't resist stopping and scanning the tables of several Indian merchants, looking for a piece of jewelry that grabs me. Among the Kachina dolls, dream catchers, necklaces, and bracelets, I finally spot a striking ring for a memento.

Lake Powell and the Glen Canyon Dam

Sand whips my eyes as I pull the Wing back onto SR 64. I'm heading for US 89,

🔊 *Down another long, plumb-line road in a breathtaking landscape.*

which will take me up to Lake Powell. The road is long and straight until it winds up towards Page. Built in 1957, as a town to house the construction workers for the massive Glen Canyon Dam project, Page has developed into a prosperous service town for Lake Powell. With several, reasonably priced hotels overlooking the southern edge of the lake, it makes a good stop for the night. But first, I'm drawn to drive another few miles to catch the sunset from an overlook along Lake Powell's blood-red cliff banks.

The views of the lake are a breathtaking contrast of the radiant blues of the Colorado River water against the carmine canyon walls. Few spots will offer more interplays of color at sunset than seen in this controversial space. To describe Lake Powell, it is said that one should imagine the Grand Canyon, and then imagine it full of water. It is a truly beautiful place.

But the Glen Canyon Dam also bears the stigma of being an extreme example of environmental pillaging. Starving the canyons below the dam of the natural flow of the Colorado River drastically changed an environment that was very sensitive to the delicate balance of water

provided by the only water source. Edward Abbey, the longtime Southwestern environmental champion, based his most well known novel, *The Monkey-Wrench Gang*, on a fictitious plot to blow up the dam. Over the decades since its completion in 1963, the dam has been the focus of a heated battle pitting advocates decrying the scarcity of water and energy for Phoenix, Las Vegas, and Los Angeles against environmentalists demanding the canyon be returned to its natural state. Those who remember Glen Canyon before the damming profess it was as beautiful as the Grand Canyon itself.

The lake claims almost 2,000 miles of coastline – more than the U.S. has on the Pacific Coast. Dammed in 1963 and fed by the constant Colorado River flow, it still took *17 years* to fill. Vacationers rent houseboats and tool around from spot to spot beside the colorful sandstone cliffs. Canoes and kayaks slip deep into slot-canyons so narrow there isn't room to turn around.

The Vermillion Cliffs Loop

Early the next morning, I continue up US 89 into Utah and Vermillion Cliffs National Monument. This loop will circle me back to Page in a few hours, but it

can't be skipped because it is one the most gorgeous rides in the Southwest. From Vermillion Cliffs, I ride through the Pariah Canyon and then to Grand Staircase-Escalante National Monument. Huge sweepers wind around the hilly formations of soil and shale erosion. The colors of the sediment layers through this stretch of US 89 through southern Utah are as vibrant and varied as any in Arizona, and I have the road almost to myself. The speedometer creeps higher and higher. The foot pegs begin to hit the pavement as I lean the Gold Wing lower into 20-second sweepers with the additional speed. Giant cliffs rise above me on the northern side, and far in the distance to the south lie the hilltops that climb into the Kaibab National Forest on the North Rim of the Grand Canyon. Joining alternate US 89 in Fredonia, the road makes a U-turn that will take me back to Page through the Kaibab.

The road travels straight over the flat plateau on its way to the knobby hilltops in the distance. Here it begins to wrap its way towards Jacob Lake, an alpine village where SR 67 will take visitors south to the North Rim of the Canyon. Unfortunately, the North Rim doesn't open until mid-May because of snow, and so it was off-limits for me on this trip. But the winding, lonely roads through the trees of the Kaibab more than made up for my bad timing. The climactic moment of this loop comes as alternate US 89 heads out of the Kaibab down into the flat top of the plateau. Three or four hairpins in a row drop me abruptly out of the elevated trees onto the flat plateau below. I have to stop and catch my breath before returning to Navajo country.

Navajoland and
the Hopi Reservation

Once again I approach Page but turn right on SR 98 just before town. I'm headed to Tuba City, one of the Navajo Nation's larger towns. As the rock outcroppings and cliff formations slide by, I'm overcome by an urge to stop and walk off the road onto the red dirt. A couple hundred yards into a natural amphitheater, I stand in silence. The sun throws a long shadow off a cliff to the west and the filtered light of late afternoon brightens the reds and oranges of a cliff to the east. The complete absence of sound is odd and disorienting, and I begin to walk just to hear the sound of my footsteps.

This is the northwestern corner of Navajoland, where the rock formations of the Painted Desert suggest the supernatural. The Navajo religion centers on the Earth People, ordinary mortals, and the Holy People, invisible spirits who help or hurt the Earth People.

In Tuba City, I arrive and check into a Quality Inn beside the historic Tuba City Trading Post, which has been around since 1870. There aren't many places to stay here, but the Quality Inn is very nice and has lots of early photographs from the area as well as a collection of interesting wall maps and artifacts in the lobby and halls.

The next morning, after a Navajo frybread breakfast, I'm headed east on SR 264 through the heart of the Hopi Indian Reservation. In the center of the Navajo Nation, buffered from the influence of the modern American way of life, it manages to preserve a sacred, resolute heritage. The Hopi story is one of determined resistance to the ways of the white man, and to this day, only three of the twelve

villages have adopted anything close to a western form of governance. The others maintain the traditional Hopi forms of social function. One of these, Old Oraibi, has even refused all funds and assistance from the Hopi Tribal Council (which receives and distributes U.S. funds) in its attempt to carry on the traditional Hopi lifestyle.

I decide to stop in at Old Oraibi, although I had read that white visitors are sometimes unwelcome. Old Oraibi shops offer genuine Kachina dolls and examples of Hopi silversmithing that often feature a unique technique known as Hopi overlay. Upon arrival, I find an ancient-looking pueblo town no larger than a couple of city blocks. No electricity services the town. Signs posted

↻ *Any notions of our significance certainly pale amid this grandeur.*

♪ *The Colorado River is the vein of life for millions of people.*

warn not to walk anywhere near the *kivas* (Hopi ceremonial rooms), or to take any photographs. I find no hostility – just a friendly shopkeeper and artisan displaying the local wares. The town has an air of peacefulness – a feeling of happiness in its isolation – and it comforts me that such an ancient culture has managed to survive to such an extent.

Old Oraibi and nearby Walpi are the two oldest continuously inhabited villages in North America. They date back to the ninth century, and the traditional way of life is a direct link to the ancient societies that had thrived here for nearly 10,000 years.

I begin heading south on SR 87 from Second Mesa. First, Second, and Third Mesa are thought by the Hopi to be the center of the universe, the place where all life began. This 2.5 million acres is the heart of the original Hopi *tutsqua*, a term meaning territory, and it's all that's left of what is believed to have encompassed 18 million acres. Soon, I'm back into the southern edge of Navajo country on a grassy plain where massive stone cliffs rise on the horizon.

About 50 miles after exiting the Nation's border one comes to I-40 at Winslow. The town's claim to fame is a mention in The Eagles song "Take It Easy" – 'Well, I'm standin' on a corner in Winslow, Arizona…' The town hypes this connection to rock-and-roll with a statue and a mural with the lyric inscribed on the main corner downtown where you can wait around for that girl in the "flat-bed Ford" or continue south on SR 87 toward the Mogollon Rim and the distant mountain ranges.

One last windy stretch of road brings me into the mountains again as I head northwest on SR 64 back into Flagstaff, with the frozen summit of Humphrey's Peak visible for miles on the approach.

Northern Arizona is a spiritual place. The scale of the Grand Canyon's immensity, the changes wrought over eons, broadcasts the power of nature loudly and clearly, and the sight stripped bare any thoughts of my significance. But the Hopi and Navajo live in quiet harmony with that same awareness, quite happy to be a part of something larger and much more enduring than they are. 🜨

↻ *In Arizona, all roads seem to lead to incredibly stunning scenery.*

FACTS AND INFORMATION

Total Mileage

Approximately 823 miles.

In General

The three main areas of Northern Arizona to be considered for a motorcycle trip are the Grand Canyon area (including Vermillion Cliffs and Grand Staircase-Escalante National Monument), the Navajo and Hopi lands, and the Monument Valley area. Be prepared for living lessons in ancient history and grand-scale geology.

Travel Season

As in most of Arizona, the climate can be very unpredictable. Located on top of the Colorado Plateau, most of Northern Arizona is much cooler than the desert expanses to the south. Still, summers and winters have their extremes. Early and late summer is the most comfortable time to visit. There are few guarantees beyond this.

Roads & Biking

Wide sweepers intertwine with the predominantly long and straight stretches of roads in this region of Arizona. The area is well paved with little traffic, except for routes near the Grand Canyon, and offers viewpoints with unparalleled scenery along the way.

Food & Lodging

Although gas and lodging are expensive in Northern Arizona, food is fairly inexpensive. Finding a good Navajo restaurant can be a real treat. If you have the skill and knowledge, camping in these areas is a lot of fun, inexpensive and reliable (campgrounds are everywhere).

Maps

○ *Arizona Atlas & Gazetteer*, Delorme Publishing, ISBN 0899333257, $19.95

○ *Rand McNally Folded Map: Flagstaff, Sedona* Rand McNally & Company ISBN 0528867571, $4.95

○ *Rand McNally EasyFinder Map: Arizona*, Rand McNally & Company ISBN 052899719X, $7.95

More Information

○ Flagstaff Convention Center & Visitors Bureau www.flagstaffarizona.org

○ Arizona Office of Tourism www.arizonaguide.com

Attractions

❶ Kaibab National Forest (928) 635-8200

❷ Museum of Northern Arizona (928) 774-5213

❸ Lowell Observatory (928) 774-3358

❹ Grand Canyon National Park General Visitor Information (928) 638-7888

❺ Colorado River Discovery (Glen Canyon Dam) (928) 645-9175

❻ Navajo Nation: Old Oraibi

❼ Grand Staircase-Escalante National Monument (435) 644-4300

❽ Navajo National Monument (928) 672-2700

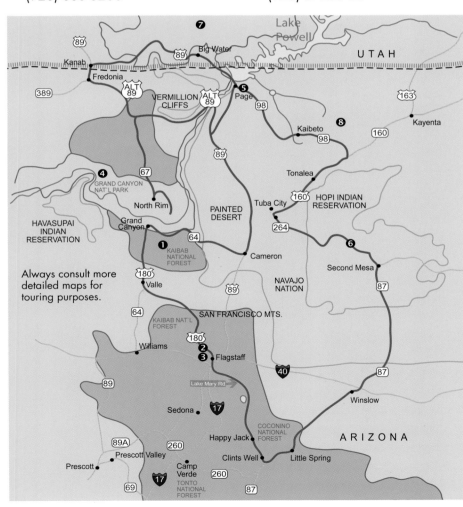

Always consult more detailed maps for touring purposes.

The Southwest

Santa Fe Trails

High-Country Harley Escapade

With only three days to spare for exploration, the choice of Santa Fe and its exhilarating surroundings is a wise one. The weather is fine and the way unwinds as smoothly as silk beneath our Road Kings.

Text and Photography: Christian Neuhauser

A number of people have asked me recently to define a shamrock tour. Simply put, it's an exploration of the roads in an area that branch off in three or four directions – like the leaves of a shamrock or clover – from a central location (usually a small town). On this trip, we spent a few days cruising our shamrock in a different way, and chose a much larger site than normal – Santa Fe, the capital of New Mexico – as our base of operations.

The Turquoise Bear

At two in the afternoon Mike Miller, an old friend, and I arrive in the sauna called Albuquerque. I'm curious and a little anxious because this occasion marks a baptism of sorts – it's my first time touring upon a Harley.

An hour on, we enter the city limits of Santa Fe and I pull over, interrupting our smooth ride for a moment to consult the map. My companion Mike uses the opportunity to sing the praises of his Road King. I quickly find our way "home," to the Inn of the Turquoise Bear. Five minutes later we turn onto the driveway of this inviting adobe Bed & Breakfast. And when reporting on our safe arrival to my wife, I didn't forget to tell her what a great job she did finding our lodgings in this historic home on the old Santa Fe Trail.

The First Big Leaf:
Indians and
Mushroom Clouds

A big breakfast with mounds of fresh fruit, freshly baked breads, and delicious coffee amply prepares us for the first day's giant leaf, a 265-mile tour. Robert Frost and Ralph Bolton, the inn's owners, wish us luck and we're out the door.

The Harleys purr in the early morning breeze. It's cold, actually a bone-chilling cold, undoubtedly because Santa Fe's elevation is approximately 6,400 feet. We take 285 to Pojoaque and later, on 4, we swing the wide sweepers to the Bandelier National Monument.

For those with three to four hours at their disposal to wander the fascinating dwellings carved from the tuff-covered cliffs and the other site remains of the Pueblo culture here, the entrance fee to Bandelier is only $12. We decided to pass it by this time out, but hope to come again to explore where the peaceful Anasazi people lived and turned the fertile soil (growing corn, beans, and squash) along Frijoles Creek some 700 to 450 years ago. At some point, they moved to the base of the cliffs and erected a communal house called Tyuonyi, a two-story, freestanding masonry pueblo with 400 rooms. Combinations of famine, drought, and soil-eroding flash floods eventually drove the tribe out, and by 1550 they had resettled along the Rio Grande. Today, a 1.5-mile paved loop trail leads past the cliff dwellings and restored ruins.

We take a turn on 502 to Los Alamos, a town that marks two widely dispersed eras of destruction. In the 1500s, Spanish explorers found nearly eighty pueblos scattered along the Rio Grande and the decimation of these Indians began; 400 years later the first atomic bomb detonated on July 16, 1945, in the pre-dawn desert at Trinity Site, 60 miles north of Alamogordo. When we consider all this and I look into Mike's serious face, I see some-

♦ Smooth cruising on Hwy 38 to Red River.   *➲ Getting the best of Sandia Crest: Downhill derring-do.*

thing else and can't help but laugh. The sun at this elevation can be very dangerous, and once Mike removed his goggles the damage is obvious. He looks like a raccoon.

Back on 502 we speed back to Hwy 4 through the Jemez Mountains. A very curvy, bumpy road leads us to Jemez Springs. Another interesting stretch of contrasts: on one side we see acres of charred sticks and on the other a wonderful, lush green meadow. An enormous wildfire destroyed a great portion of these woods. But, looking the other way, I wouldn't have been surprised to see a band of buffalo-hunting Indians. Hitting Jemez Springs just in time for a lunch, we cruise into parking spots at Deb's Deli. Just so you know, the ice cream is really good.

After reloading with grub, we hit Hwy 4 toward San Ysidro, where we take Hwy 550: primarily two lanes built for racing. Flying to Cuba, bonding with the wide curves, I lose the raccoon in my mirror, turn around, and retrace the trail to find him pacing a parking lot. He's very agitated.

"What's up my friend?" I ask.

"My Harley died," his ominous reply. A bad situation in a remote area.

♁ *Roving the adobe in downtown Santa Fe.*

I walk around the bike and chuckle again. "You touched the kill button." Swinging into our saddles, we take on Hwy 96 and 84, returning to Santa Fe.

Second Loop:
Loneliness and Wildfires

The sun blinks our wake-up. Can we expect another fine day in this sector of biker paradise?

It's cold again but there's nothing but deep blue, cloudless sky ahead. In Espanola we follow route 68 to Taos, where the unrelenting miles of polar blast finally get the best of us. We have to stop. Coffee is my salvation, and the waitress keeps it coming. Mike enjoys his hot chocolate and we warm up slowly. The view of snow-capped mountains reminds us we should have expected a little brush with hypothermia – after all, we are touring an alpine area. Wheeler Peak, the highest point in New Mexico, at 13,161 feet, greets us with its frigid face.

Taos certainly doesn't shy from its designation as a tourist trap. They overcharge for everything. Ten bucks to enter the pueblo is okay, I guess, but five dollars again for a photo permit is a rip. Winding along Hwy 38, my rancor gradually recedes on the way to Red River. We stop at Frye's Old Town. A colorful western-style facade invites us to visit the country store. One of the employees there hears Mike's southern accent and recommends a barbeque restaurant just around the corner, where they serve us a mean lunch of sliced pork that practically melts on our tongues.

♁ *The Taos Pueblo.*

On to our next target – Bobcat Pass at 9,854 ft. A smooth road leads us to the top before we sweep down to Eagles Nest and Angel Fire. Following that we get onto 434, probably the loneliest road in this area. Curvy and sometimes a one-lane serpent, it travels along the Sangre de Cristo Mountains to Mora. I enjoy this portion a great deal, wave to Mike, and open the throttle. Arcing the Road King through the curves, I still feel comfortable with the easy handling.

In Mora, Route 518 offers other surprises, some of which are wholly unexpected. Wide sweepers and great asphalt naturally opens the throttle again – going 55 mph, sometimes a bit more, I swing toward Vadito. But what is this smell? Is something wrong with my Harley? No, there must be a fire. A few miles later on Hwy 76 south we see roiling clouds of smoke on the horizon. This road is a wild ride of ups and downs and fast changing turns, but we are too concerned about the wildfire to enjoy it very much. Hundreds of people line the road watching. We stop, too, and learn the fire is near Nambe. The wind is coming from the southwest, which means Santa Fe is not in danger, and it's too loud to hear

yourself think. Huge tanker planes loaded with chemical flame retardant rumble overhead. It's a dangerous, mesmerizing spectacle, and I'm saddened by the losses of the harried people among us.

The wildfire has reached 600 acres and is not yet under control, I hear the correspondent saying on the tube when I exit the shower. The ride back was great, but under the circumstances our thoughts were more with the firefighters and the victims.

Last Leaf:
Madrid & Sandia Crest

Early in the morning we push the buttons and the Harleys hum without missing a beat.

Cruising 14 is a good way to start an early morning tour. Smooth, but not too challenging, the road winds toward Madrid. We've encountered red soil, cliffs, high mountains, and evergreen forests. Today, it's a course in plains riding like the Pony Express and the only thing of consequence that we can make out on the horizon is a big hill growing larger – Sandia Crest.

But first we stop the Harley Express in Madrid, a small and isolated artists

colony. We grab some coffee and water, and roam awhile to take in an atmosphere typical of the late 1960s. A good general store is essential in the middle of nowhere and the one in Madrid sells practically everything. And the feeling of walking through a time warp even extends to their jukebox: The Mamas and Papas. "Ca-li-for-nia, Ca-li-for-nia dreaming…"

"Let's ride, my friend," Mike says, finally reminding me we have something to do, and after a couple of miles we reach this Something. The intersection to Sandia Crest is a smooth right turn, but I have a premonition it's the last smooth turn. Two miles later the road screws up to the top of the mountain. I whiz through the curves and sometimes the footrest nicks the asphalt. I like that, and after what seems like hundreds of switchbacks, a small parking lot welcomes us at the end of the road. Sandia Crest: 10,678 feet.

The air is thin, the breathing is hard, and the view is exhilarating. Mountains, plains, desert, and woodlands. You can see almost two-thirds of New Mexico from here. The wildfire still burns; it looks even larger. When we started our climb, the temperature was 89 degrees; at the top, it's only 52 degrees. That's a new experience for me. So be careful when you choose your outfit for outings like this. Now we have the same road again. The downhill race begins. The only things I wish for now are better brakes. And from time to time you need luck, too. Today, thankfully, I'm on the sunny side of the street.

Back in Santa Fe by three, we pick up our luggage and hit the road for Albuquerque. Our three-day tour is over, and already we would like to come again. It was such a great and unforgettable experience. ⬤

↻ *Red River, New Mexico.*

FACTS AND INFORMATION

Total Mileage

Approximately 671 miles.

In General

Nestled between the Sangre de Cristo Range (Wheeler Peak –13,161 ft.) and the Sandia Crest mountain (10,760 ft.), Santa Fe sits 7,200 feet above sea level. The surrounding area is rich in Native-American culture, mainly the Pueblo Indians, and the influence of Spanish explorers. Adobe structures predominate downtown and in many of the surrounding residential areas.

Today, Santa Fe is a popular residence for national and international artists. You'll find great galleries, beautiful accommodations, and enjoy delicious Southwestern fare.

Travel Season

The best travel season is between May and October, when dry, sunny days are a good probability. Due to the change in altitudes (from 3,000 to 13,000 feet) temperatures can vary from a toasty 92° F in Albuquerque to a comfortable 70° F in Chama on the same day during the summer. Rains usually arrive in the form of afternoon thunderstorms, which unleash torrents and frequently cause flash flooding. Campers shouldn't pitch tents along streambeds here. The combination of intense sun and high altitude makes daily sunscreen use a necessity.

Roads & Biking

The roads are in great condition, the asphalt has good grip, and you can find wide sweepers as well as narrow turns in the surrounding area. The road to Angel Fire towards Mora (Hwy 434) is narrow and twisty, but stay alert for deer. The same goes for 96 between Gallina and the intersection of Hwy 84.

Food & Lodging

The Santa Fe area thrives on tourism, and you'll find all sorts of motel chains, private motels, Bed & Breakfasts, and upscale resorts. Some restaurants and lodgings are expensive, but there are many nice places where the balance between the quality offered and the price asked is most agreeable.

Maps

o *New Mexico Map*
  Rand McNally
  ISBN 978-0528998614, $4.95
o AAA *Arizona/New Mexico*
  State Series Map

More Information

o New Mexico Tourism Department
  www.newmexico.org
o Santa Fe, New Mexico
  www.santafe.com
o Red River, New Mexico
  www.redriver.org

Attractions

❶ Bandelier National Monument
  (505) 672-3861 x 517
❷ The Taos Pueblo, (575) 758-1028
❸ Frye's Old Town, (505) 754-6165
❹ Jemez State Monument
  (505) 829-3530
❺ Pecos National Historical Park
  (505) 757-6414 x 1
❻ Battleship Rock & McCauley
  Hot Springs

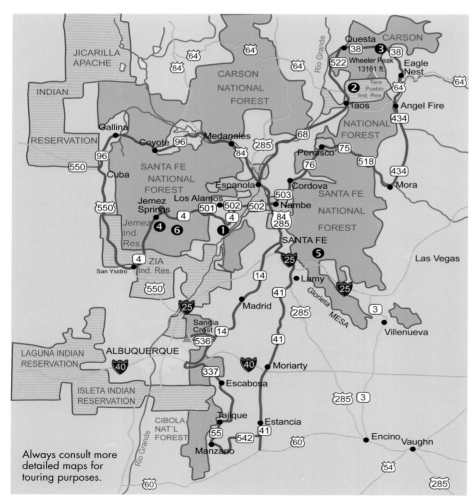

Always consult more detailed maps for touring purposes.

Packing a Bike

The books went first, in Paris… But not until Athens was on the horizon did the evening clothes, the dancing slippers and even the immaculately white mess jacket go overboard. In London, it had seemed impossible to travel without proper evening clothes. One could see an invitation arriving for an embassy ball or something… But on the other side of Europe embassy balls held less significance.

— Robert Edison Fulton Jr.,
One Man Caravan, 1937

The most useful advice I ever got about travel in general was "Take half as many clothes and twice the money!"

And while credit cards have rendered that advice partly obsolete, the first item still applies. The best way to pack those "just in case" items is to leave them at home, just as Robert Edison Fulton discovered. Or you can plan to lighten the load as you go. The general principle here, is pack only what you need. If you think you won't need it, don't take it. This doesn't apply to rain gear, essential tools or safety equipment, of course.

Second, while you want to keep your load as light as possible, you can reduce the negative impacts of surplus weight on your bike by keeping it as close as possible to the center of gravity. That means putting heavier items in side bags (panniers) rather than in a top box, tail pack or tank bag. Top boxes and tail packs, as well as being well above the bike's center of gravity, are typically behind the rear axle.

Extra inertia above the center of gravity will make the bike slower to lean and therefore slower to turn at speed. More importantly, it will be slower to straighten up, too! The weight behind the rear axle will lighten the front end, further upsetting the bike's balance. Keep heavy stuff down low. Or don't take it.

The extra weight high up will also make your bike more inclined to tip over at low speed. And, unless it was designed as an integral part of the bike (on a Gold Wing for example), a top box may upset your bike's aerodynamics. I only use a top box when I really have to.

⌂ *Keep the heavier items packed and balanced as low as possible.*

A tank bag is a great place to keep things you want easy access to, and almost all have a map pocket so you can track your route as you go. Before you buy a tank bag, though, find out what your gas tank (or dummy tank airbox cover) is made of. Magnetic bags are best, but they only work on steel.

Hard luggage is generally preferable to soft throw-over bags, but the latter are more flexible – literally! They transfer easily from bike to bike and can accommodate irregularly shaped objects. Just remember to protect any contacting bodywork with masking tape.

From here, the general principles of packing are mostly common sense:

Take plastic bags. Use them to store laundry, food, maps or anything that might leak or contaminate other items. I always take heavy-grade Ziplock® freezer bags.

Don't overload your bike. Follow the manufacturer's guidelines for weight. And keep in mind: if it won't fit in your luggage, you've probably packed too much stuff!

Allow for expansion. I always seem to acquire things as I go, like T-shirts, maps and books. Leave some room.

Remember also you may need room for stuff you're wearing if the temperature rises and you need to dress down. Overpants, vests and jacket liners, for example.

Take bungee cords and an elastic cargo net for unexpected extra purchases – and plastic bags to stuff them in.

Pack the stuff you'll need in a hurry (first aid kit, raingear, etc.) on top, or in your tank bag.

Develop a packing checklist. Add items you discovered you needed but didn't have, and vice versa. But always carry drinking water, sunscreen, mobile phone or CB radio, credit card and a puncture kit.

Finally, adjust your tire pressures and suspension settings to allow for the extra loading. Take it easy for the first few miles until you get used to the extra weight.

Learn from every trip to become more efficient at packing your bike.

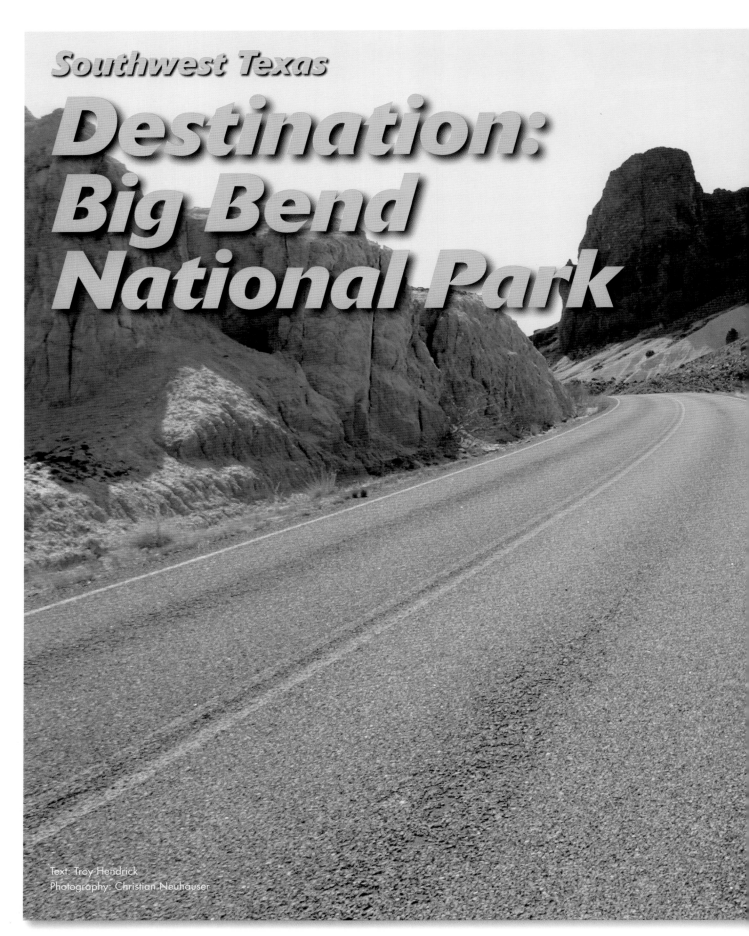

Southwest Texas
Destination: Big Bend National Park

Text: Troy Hendrick
Photography: Christian Neuhauser

This land is beautiful and cruel. Cacti and creosote dot the ground and bloom from the road's edge to the far horizon. Long, sharp spines flare from the waxy stems, ready to draw blood.

We go from one extreme to another – desert roads that never seem to end to green vistas of misty mountains. From blazing heat to bone-chilling cold. From a grand river to a parched desert. Riding in southwest Texas is certainly no day at the beach, but its reputation as a top-notch riding destination warrants investigation.

So far, fighting wind, rain, and heat on US 90, we aren't impressed. My KTM Adventure LC4 enduro seems a match for the landscape, and Christian rides comfortably on his Agusta MZ, but these roads are so long and straight. The fun must be hidden elsewhere. Finally, we arrive in Del Rio, an Air Force town, where the jet fighters that streaked the horizon throughout the day are based. Population: 40,000, many of them servicemen, and a fair portion of those are venting some steam in their cowboy hats and boots,

dancing with the ladies in the bar across the street from our rooms at the La Quinta Inn. The map still shows a full day's ride to Big Bend National Park and, unfortunately, the dot of Del Rio appears to be the only major oasis along the way.

The first test of our mettle comes the second morning. Just out of Del Rio, we cross the Amistad Reservoir. Christian signals a stop at an overlook for some photos on the rocky shores of the blue-green lake. Rolling the bikes onto some rocks beside a boat ramp, we take the shots, and I start the KTM and move her back up to the lot. But the MZ won't crank. After some uneducated speculation about the cause, we use the KTM to jump the MZ, which gives the battery enough juice to flush a small flood, and it rumbles to life. Later, we learn that the fuel line should be turned off, even for very brief stops. Hot and frustrated, we push forward.

I have to wring sweat out of my T-shirt at every stop. As we head toward the afternoon sun, the road seems endless. Thoughts of an air-conditioned room are little comfort as I watch the heat-wavering horizon remain constant for hours.

Finally, a few roads intersect in the town of Sanderson. The squelch of metal scraping metal on a sign swinging in the wind at the gas station is the only sound. I almost expect to turn and face the unblinking eye of a buzzard. There is definitely no lodging here, but the attendant tells us to check in the next town over, Marathon. In these parts, getting to 'the next town over' might as well be a marathon.

Within twenty minutes of leaving Sanderson, the sun hits the horizon, the temperature drops 40 degrees, and a numbing tingle crawls up my hands and feet. After so much smothering heat, this frigid air is shocking. Counting each mile to Marathon, both of us wary, we open

🜂 *Resting among the pinyon pines at the base of the Davis Mountains.*

the throttles and race the cold. I grit my teeth and look for the lights of Marathon over each rise. Eventually we coast onto its main street in moonlight. Parking in front of a handsome lodge, Christian goes inside to check on a room. He's told that it's full. Our frustration heightens when we come upon the only other option's NO VACANCY sign; so we continue to Alpine, another 35 minutes west. Shivering and hungry, we finally get a room, and thankfully the restaurant across the street is open. At the end of two days, the Texas desert is laying on a beating, but we've finally reached the gateway to Big Bend National Park, and after all we've been through, getting here is no small accomplishment. Spicy beef taquitos in a warm family restaurant begin to heal us, and though fatigued we're excited over the prospect of finally reaching our goal and exploring an area that is so well protected by the desert.

We need a good laugh to raise our spirits before riding into the park, and I provide one around four a.m. I awake to answer nature's call and returned in total darkness to my bed, or so I thought. I have been in a thousand motel rooms, and most are the same. But this one, like most things in Texas, is much bigger than most. Leaning forward, hands extended, expecting to land on my mattress and crawl under the covers, I feel a vertiginous instant of panic as I slowly lean into nothing. After crashing headfirst into the nightstand, ricocheting into the side of my bed, and coming to rest on the carpet, I mumble some self-directed insults and wearily haul myself between the sheets. Other than a bruised ego, I wake with a skinned knee and a tender bump on my head big enough for Christian to see. I tried to keep it from him, but he coaxed the story and got plenty of mileage out of it over the next few days. He just couldn't resist. ("Troy, you'd better make sure that chair is under you before you try to sit down," etc., etc.).

The chill of a brisk desert night has yet to burn away as we follow State Road 118 south to the big bend in the Rio Grande that lends the national park its name. Massive sandstone buttes, like petrified dunes, rise from the level desert floor and cast immense shadows that are painfully cold to ride through. Where the road cuts through clusters of bluffs, there are plenty of sweepers and twisties to negotiate, and the riding is starting to live up to its reputation. Signs on the road identify distant shapes with names like Packsaddle Mountain, Hen Egg Mountain, and Butcherknife Hill.

Finally, we reach the park's entrance. The sun has just begun the daily baking process, but our gas tanks are full and we're grinning at a winding road leading into a breathtaking landscape. The hills and buttes have graduated to legitimate mountain ranges, and the entrance road steers right into the heart of them.

These steep, spiny mountains belong to the Chisos Range, where some peaks reach over 7,000 feet. Combined with the desert climate below, this range nurtures a very unique ecosystem. One of the Big Bend's distinctions is that it is home to more species of birds than anywhere else in North America due to the area's striking individuality and diversity. We're climbing toward the park's central headquarters, the temperature is balmy at the higher elevation, the views are thrilling, and we've forgiven southwest Texas for all its adversity.

Down from the mountains and closer to the river on the southern border of the park (and the nation), the climate changes dramatically. It's open desert again, but splashes of bright green vegetation cling

TOP: A friendly chat outside Terlingua's dusty Starlight Theatre.
MIDDLE: Late-afternoon light casts immense shadows from the park's great sandstone cliffs.
BOTTOM: The long arm of the law still saddles up in Presidio, Texas.

◑ *Gazing upon the Rio Grande from the River Road instills a sense of the great valley we've been traversing.*

to empty streambeds, and, every once in a while, a lonely cottonwood offers a blessed circle of shade in the scorching landscape. Finally, we're on the banks of the Rio Grande, standing on a cliff high above the lime-green waters. The roads are fun to ride, and traffic isn't a problem, but we're held back a bit by the National Park Service speed limit: 35 mph.

◐ *A teepee-cal Texas desert shelter.*

The KTM Adventure is built for this country, and since I'm a former dirt biker turned street rider, I'm excited as we turn onto 14 miles of dirt, sand, and gravel. It's not necessary for every tour to the Big Bend to ride on unpaved roads, but we're giving the bikes a complete test. After a thorough coating of red dust, we reconnect with the entrance road and exit the park heading west to Terlingua. Known as a genuine ghost town, Terlingua is structured to lure the Big Bend tourists, and there is a nice café at its center. We're too late for lunch, though, and continue through the bare, rocky hills to Lajitas on Ranch Road 170. We then intersect with the River Road, winding along the banks of the Rio Grande to Presidio. The curves twist and turn along the U.S. side of the riverbank, Mexico is a stone's throw across, and the river meanders peacefully through the no man's land in the middle. I'm chasing Christian along the twisty road, loving every turn and sweeper, climbing high above the Rio Grande and swooping back down to its banks. No rider in Big Bend should miss the River Road.

In Presidio, where a policewoman sits on her horse at a gas station, we stop for a burger before heading back north to Alpine by way of US 67. I retire that evening exhausted but contented with our day in the Big Bend and carefully study the dimensions and placement of my bed. We've made up for some early mishaps, and the Big Bend tour has become well worth our troubles.

The following morning, stomachs and tanks filled, we aim for the Davis Mountains. Today's ride is the pinnacle of our tour; but, of course, it wouldn't feel like the southwest Texas we've come to know without a few minor setbacks thrown in. Riding north on SR 118, and turning west on SR 17 at Ft. Davis, we're slammed by hefty gusts that whip us all over the road. This is prairie land, much more moist and green, but there's nothing around to prevent the wind from gaining speed and momentum before it creams us. We ride low under the fairings and shove back to maintain a straight line. Turning onto SR 166, climbing into the Davis Mountain Range to escape the wind, we halt when the asphalt stops. A construction flagman holds up our ride over the next nine miles of wet, unpaved dirt. We stand around the bikes as oncoming vehicles are led past and joke about who's collecting more mud. Christian hooks some wet muck off my bike in demonstration and flicks it at me. Our minor misadventures are just another aspect of a rough landscape, and today we're taking whatever southwest Texas throws at us in stride.

The Davis Mountains are an unexpected joy that makes the whole trip worthwhile — massive pillars of stone rise out of the forest of pinyon pine and jut through cloud mist to form a fantastic image of islands in the sky. Only one camper-van slows us for a mile or two before we pass.

We turn east on SR 118, where Christian informs me the landscape resembles Sardinia, and head back to Ft. Davis. The road gracefully twists among huge boulders, alongside winding brooks in the airy

Here, where sandstone buttes predominate, the road is our only connection to civilization.

shade of the pinyon forest, and swerves around the feet of the great pillars that appear to hang like mobiles from the clouds. The McDonald Observatory takes advantage of the wide horizons and the absence of city lights here, and we stop for a quick look at the huge telescope before gliding into Ft. Davis for lunch and our preparations to fly back east.

This little corner of Texas can be mean and it doesn't need any provocation to rare back and beat the heck out of you. But inevitably, it yields a diverse majesty and elegance that makes any of those struggles worthwhile. After all, we're no worse for the wear — that is, if you don't count a scarred knee and bruised head from falling into a phantom bed.

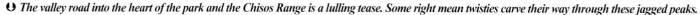

The valley road into the heart of the park and the Chisos Range is a lulling tease. Some right mean twisties carve their way through these jagged peaks.

Southwest Texas
FACTS AND INFORMATION

Total Mileage
Approximately 681 miles.

In General
The area of southwest Texas cradling the Big Bend National Park is remote, so only the most devoted tourists make the trip. Although tough to get to, the dedicated rider will be rewarded with thinly populated roads, an immense landscape untouched by modernity, and the joy of discovering a wild, beautiful sector of the American West.

Travel Season
The climate is warm year-round and roads don't close for winter conditions as in other high-altitude destinations. Fall and spring are hot but bearable, and summer temperatures can easily climb to 110° F at the base of the mountains. The best time to plan a trip is late March through May, when the desert is filled with stunning colors.

Roads & Biking
The can't-miss, have-to-ride road in the Big Bend National Park area is Ranch Road 170, also known as the River Road because it meanders beside the Rio Grande. The asphalt in the park and on the River Road is in excellent condition, but riders should note there are many dips, making sport suspensions a bit more dangerous. On SR 166, the Davis Mountains presented us with our favorite roads of the tour, providing huge sweepers, with one coming right after another.

Maps
- *Texas Road Map & Travel Guide* National Geographic Maps ISBN 159775059X, $7.95
- *Texas Official Travel Map* Texas Department of Transportation www.dot.state.tx.us/travel

More Information
- Marfa Chamber of Commerce www.marfacc.com
- Fort Davis Chamber of Commerce www.fortdavis.com
- All Across Texas www.allacrosstexas.com

Attractions
❶ National Parks Service-Big Bend National Park (432) 477-2251
❷ Historic Terlingua Ghost Town (432) 371-2234
❸ McDonald Observatory Visitors Center (432) 426-3640
❹ Gage Hotel (800) 884-4243
❺ Seminole Canyon State Park & Historic Site (432) 292-4464

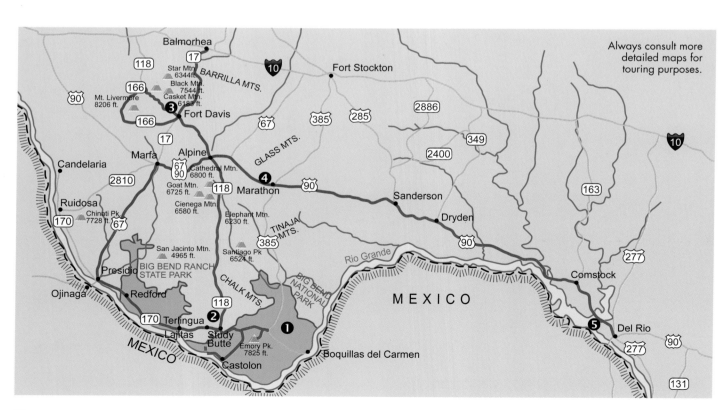

The Right Tools

There are those who say all you need in your toolbox are a credit card and a cell phone. That's fine if you're traveling on the Interstate or in well-populated areas. Otherwise, it makes sense to carry what you need to fix a minor breakdown. From my experience, the best you can expect from AAA is a lift to the nearest bike shop.

How much to carry depends on three factors: where I'm going (considering the terrain and how far it is from civilization), what I'm riding, and how long I'll be away. For example, useful as it would have been, I wouldn't have thought to take along a spare clutch lever on my island daytrip – I wasn't traveling that far and there are plenty of Yamaha dealers in British Columbia. On the other hand, on a recent trip to Baja California, I carried both spare clutch and brake levers, knowing that a tip-over was likely and that finding BMW parts in the Baja could be a challenge.

Statistically, the breakdown you're most likely to suffer on a modern motorcycle is a flat; carrying a puncture repair kit always makes sense. This will fix most flats and get you as far as a bike store for a professional repair. And while the CO2 cartridges in a puncture kit might get you going, it's unlikely they'll provide enough air for your correct pressure. So a small electric air pump and a pressure gauge are also parts of my wilderness kit.

Know your bike

On that note, it's also worth carrying any special tools you might need to remove a wheel. For example, my Triumph Sprint ST uses a single 46mm nut to secure the rear wheel. I've never yet found a bike shop, other than a Triumph dealer, that has a suitable socket. Sure, you can use a crescent wrench to get the wheel off, but doing that can damage the nut. Not a good idea. So I always carry a 46mm socket on the ST.

Most of the newer bikes are designed to run with semi or full synthetic oil and finding motorcycle grade synthetic anywhere but a bike shop is a hopeless quest. You can use regular oil in a pinch, but I only put the best "dino juice" in my babies. That's why I carry a quart of the good stuff for emergencies.

If your bike uses a cable-operated clutch or throttle, carry a spare. When possible, tape it to the existing cable, and that way, a quick swap is all you have to do in the event a cable lets go.

Anything else?

Your bike may have came with a tool kit, but don't assume it contains what you need. Many of the tools will be made from cheese or modeling clay, at best. The 17mm wrench provided to adjust the chain on my ST was good for but one use before it was hopelessly rounded, so now I carry a 17mm combination wrench.

Modern electrical systems are highly sophisticated and rarely give trouble; but light bulbs are still prone to failure. I always carry replacements for the bulbs most critical to the safe operation of my bike: headlight, stop/tail light and turn signals.

Many bikes use a large number of M6 screws with a 10mm head; so I keep a 10mm combination wrench in my toolkit for roadside adjustments. Next to it is my Gerber multi-tool. This handy item has all the usual pliers and blades, but also includes a quarter-inch square drive adapter so I can use it with sockets.

There are two more essentials that I won't travel without. A small crescent wrench will tackle most fasteners up to about a half-inch. And I keep a small pair of vise grips on board, too. I've used these for just about everything, including operating the throttle after a cable let go, holding loose parts in place – and even as an emergency shift lever! While traveling in a group, you don't all need to be carrying a complete toolkit.

The key word here is "planning." You can't cover every emergency, but you'll be able to handle most minor issues if you think through what you might need. When all else fails, there's duct tape. And for good measure, pack that credit card and cell phone, too!

The Midwest

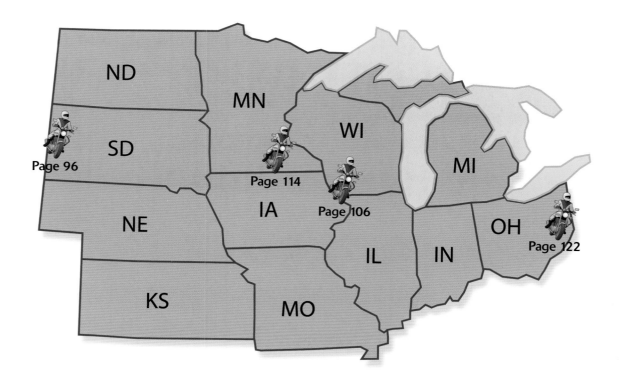

Some 50 million years ago, dry land began emerging from the shallow seas that covered most of the area between the Appalachians and the newly forming Rocky Mountains in the West. As American pioneers migrated further west in the 19th century, the area from eastern Ohio into the Great Plains states became known as the Middle West.

Today the Midwest is a land of many contrasts, topographies and scenic wonders. The Great Lakes to the area's north are huge inland freshwater seas formed by glaciers during the last Ice Age. The Great River Road follows the mighty Mississippi from its headwaters in Minnesota through America's midsection to the Gulf of Mexico.

South Dakota's Black Hills and Badlands provide visitors with unique scenery and the unforgettable image of four US Presidents carved into the granite face of Mt. Rushmore. The Ozark and Ouachita Mountains of Arkansas offer serpentine byways and interesting Ozark villages like Eureka Springs. So, "get your motors running," because we have a lot of territory to cover in the Midwest.

Black Hills,
Bison and Buttes

The biker hordes have yet to arrive for the annual Black Hills Motor Classic Rally in Sturgis, South Dakota. I have this majestic and surreal landscape mostly to myself for the next several days to explore. Buttes, bison grazing on rolling grasslands, the infamous town of Deadwood, South Dakota, historic highways and much more await my motorcycle meanderings through America's northern Great Plains.

Text and Photography: Robert Smith

♁ Grassland stretches away toward Slim Buttes.

♁ Rarely this peaceful, Cheyenne Crossing is a major weekend biker destination.

No, it wasn't bad planning on my part. It just occurred to me that being one of 500,000 motorcycles in the Black Hills might be a little overwhelming. So, arriving in June instead of August for my tour, I unload the BMW R 1200 RT, and check in to Deadwood's sumptuous Hickok's Hotel, where the historic atmosphere extends beyond all of the dark wood and period-style fittings. From my window, I have an excellent view of the mock gunfight that's staged outside on the street each night.

Sturgis

Though Deadwood nestles between steep hillsides, the 12-mile run to Sturgis is actually downhill on 14A through a dreamworld of sweepers and hairpins that turns into a traffic nightmare near the Interstate.

I head north on a straight two-lane highway to Newell, the "Sheep Capital of the USA," says the sign. (100,000 sheep are sold there annually in weekly auctions.) This is classic prairie and I could be almost anywhere in the Great Plains States with the continuously undulating landscape. The grassland is interrupted only by the occasional butte, though even these are softly rounded here, unlike the steeply ridged towering bluffs of Colorado and Utah. Arguably, Bear Butte's contours have a vaguely ursine contour, though Mud Butte is just a shallow ramble of brown hillocks. I pause by a historical marker that tells me the linear contours in the ditch next to the road are the wagon ruts made by settlers on the Bismarck-Deadwood Trail, and it also notes a massacre here, one of many in the Dakota Territory between 1876-1878, as white settlers parceled out the traditional Indian lands.

Faith is a tiny hamlet named for the daughter of the president of the Milwaukee Railroad, the line that opened up this territory to settlers. And faith is what the residents have in the rainfall that sustains their farms. The town's motto: "Next year will be better…" South toward Howes, the rolling green continues, like Ireland on steroids. They must get a lot of rain (or snow) here. Enjoying the fine grazing is a herd of buffalo – or are they bison? Apparently the North American beast is far closer related to other indigenous bovines than its distant African cousins, so bison they indeed are. Hunted close to extinction, partly as a way to deprive Plains Indians of their food supply, bison were eventually re-introduced from Canadian stock, but most modern herds are genetically impure.

Heading back toward Sturgis, I become aware of two factors: one, that at the speed I have been traveling, the

○ *A new bridge spans a ravine in Wind Cave National Park, north of Hot Springs.*

R 1200 RT guzzles gas like a 747 on takeoff; and that the miles-to-go reading on the onboard computer is not quite linear. At one point, I see I have enough fuel for 80 miles and just 40 miles to the next gas station. Then suddenly, only 40 miles worth remains, and I'm still 30 miles out! I glide into Sturgis on fumes.

Through the Gap

I turn north again, this time on the Can-Am Highway, US 85 to Belle Fourche, named by *voyageurs* for the "beautiful fork" joining the Redwater

and Belle Fourche Rivers. Nearby is the "Geographical Center of the Nation," a purely trigonometrical construct that takes into account Alaska, but conveniently not Hawaii, no doubt because otherwise the center would be out in the Pacific. In any case, reaching the "center" requires 15.6 miles of deep, coarse gravel. Tempting as it is, I decide to save that for another day.

The route north to Buffalo is quite smooth. The surrounding grassland barely undulates and Buffalo, too, is

This narrow tunnel keeps trucks and motor homes off the Needles Highway.

It takes a solid foundation to withstand the prairie winds and winter snowdrifts.

unremarkable except for a spectacular art-deco high school. Turning east on Hwy 20 toward Reva, entering Custer National Forest, I'm greeted by an abrupt canyon lined with buttes, hoodoos and standing rocks: Reva Gap. A sign promises an off-road rest area and overlook, so I ease the RT along the rutted dirt track, which soon dwindles to a single rut before fading out completely. Not wanting to ride the big Beemer into unmarked oblivion, I gingerly paddle her around and retreat to the road.

Two more excitements: turning south on 79 to Hoover, I ride over a shallow pass at Slim Buttes, where the grassland below is laid out like a green baize tablecloth. Ahead, though, I can see a storm with clouds the color of ripe plums and lightning dancing in the sky.

♎ *This pastoral scene welcomes me to Johnson Siding.*

I'm riding behind a Gray Line bus as I near the storm center and wonder if I should stick behind on the theory that the bus might be more likely to take a lightning strike. Fortunately, I just do skirt the deluge as it moves east, enduring only a short shower – and Deadwood's pavement is dry when I get back to Hickok's.

Into the Black Hills
The rain returns with a vengeance the next day, so I hunker down at Hickok's; but the following morning dawns bright and clear. I turn north out of Deadwood on 85 and I-90 Business to the 14A turnoff for Spearfish Canyon and swing through the winding ravine between soaring pine trees, steep bluffs and cascading waterfalls. With the sun just clearing the cliff tops to warm the fresh

morning air, this is the kind of ride you'd want to do every day if you lived here, yet the road is surprisingly lonely. Highway 14A terminates at the historic

stage stop of Cheyenne Crossing, and the parking lot of the diner which sits there now is usually filled with cruiser bikes on weekends. It's empty today, though.

♎ *Reva Gap appears in the distance on Highway 20.*

South on 85 toward Newcastle takes me through more meandering canyons, although I'm soon climbing over open range dotted with pine copses to the 7,000-ft O'Neill Pass. At US16, I turn east through Custer, a neatly laid out town of clean, colorful houses and tidy gardens. I'm looking for 89 North, which will connect me with the Needles Highway. Riding delights – endearingly picturesque as they wind in and out of the pine forest, smooth of surface and exquisitely curvy – both roads are lively and challenging. Some very tight uphill hairpins cause the ST to struggle: first gear is very tall and I have to gun the engine and slip the clutch aggressively to stay upright. The Needles Highway, especially, is a romping, rollicking ride along wooded slopes lined with tarmac trickery: just what motorcycles were made for.

The Needles Highway's star attraction is a tunnel that's maybe 100 feet long but only 8 feet wide, and so too narrow for motor homes. Hooray! I learn later that I have one Peter Norbeck to thank for these delightful highways. A son of Norwegian immigrants, Norbeck served the state as Lieutenant Governor (1915-1917), its ninth Governor (1917-1921) and as a U.S. Senator (1921-1936). He was largely responsible for opening up the Black Hills as a destination with interesting driving (and riding!) roads.

↻ *So that's why it's called the Needles Highway.*

↻ *A pigtail bridge, one of Peter Norbeck's engineering innovations.*

The Needles Highway butts into 89, and I cut back west to travel Custer State Park's Wildlife Loop. It's quite a devious road, with numerous blind rises (often hiding stopped cars), unmarked bends, and a poor surface. Of course, its main aim is to offer wildlife sightings, not to cater to enthusiastic motorcyclists; but even so, all I saw were three small buffalo and a sad-looking deer.

Highway 16-Alt takes me back toward Mt. Rushmore. It has so many twisties I almost get whiplash! There are more tunnels, too, and a new treat: pigtail bridges. A Norbeck innovation, these 270-degree loops allow road direction and elevation changes in the minimum amount of space. They're fun to ride, too!

My first glimpse of magnificent Mount Rushmore makes me think of *North by Northwest* and the scenes in which Cary Grant and Eva Marie Saint are clinging desperately to any handhold on those gargantuan faces. It's an impressive memorial to greatness, and as my telephoto lens reveals, the carving is sharp and intricate. For the best views, however, sightseers must gain access at the "visitors center," a plaza about the size of Disneyland, and although admission is free, there is a $10 parking fee.

Heading back to Deadwood, I take US 385. It's marked as "scenic" on my map, but really it's just a two-lane connector heavily traveled by commercial and recreational traffic.

Finding Nemo Road

The fine weather holds for another day, and I set out to ride across country to Rapid City. Nemo Road is a classic, weaving through fields and forests as it climbs into the Black (dark-green, really) Hills. Like most roads in the region, it's perfectly engineered and immaculately surfaced, too. Neither have I run into any

construction – a miracle considering what the weather must be like here in the winter. Nemo itself is a tiny farming community that was founded in 1889.

Rapid City, a cheery community of neat bungalows and clean streets, is known for its balmy microclimate, which keeps it mostly snow-free in winter while the rest of the region shivers. It's Saturday and around 9:00 a.m. when I arrive, so the garage sales are just starting up, and even their wares are tidily displayed. I stop at McDonald's and find it to be the cleanest, best

maintained, and busiest I've ever been in. The employees are well dressed and courteous, and at many tables, extended families are enjoying Saturday brunch. I wonder for a moment if I've stumbled into *Pleasantville*.

Mt. Rushmore Highway is a busy four-lane road lined with entertainment opportunities: the Reptile Gardens, Cockroach World, the Velvet Painting Museum… OK, I made up the last two, but you get the idea. Every star attraction begets attractions, and a giant patriotic sculpture is a big draw.

↻ *In stark contrast to Rally Week, mine is the only bike at the Full Throttle.*

◑ *Deadwood's bustling Main Street.*

I turn off the MRH to Keystone and start looking for the Holy Terror Highway, South Dakota 40. Apparently, one William B. Franklin staked his claim on land that became the area's best producing gold mine. Fond of his drink, Franklin was often dragged home from the saloon by his wife Jenny, about whom he was wont to say, "Ain't she a holy terror?" Also in Keystone is the National Presidential Wax Museum, which wittily claims their displays go "from George W to George W…"

I'm climbing through dense forest back into the Black Hills before the road breaks out onto prairie, ending at SD79. The turn I'm looking for, SD36, is just a few hundred yards south. It's a charming, wandering road, ambling between pine stands next to a creek,

and eventually leads to scenic 16A. It's here I turn south on SD87, which swings and sways through more pine forest before again opening onto high plateau. And in spite of the Columbian features (grazing bison, swaying grasses, pine trees), a blustery wind and the rolling terrain also bring to mind England's North Yorkshire Moors. The buffalo – sorry, bison – here are huge, like four-legged semi-trailers.

Hot Springs is a pleasant, affluent-looking riverfront town of adobe-colored stone buildings with its own downtown waterfall. I'd originally planned to take 79 back to Rapid City, but it looks unappetizingly straight and flat; so instead I retrace 385 to check out some more of the Black Hills roads, like 44, the Rim Rock Scenic Highway going east from Silver City – and I'm

really glad I did! It's a playground of fast sweeping bends that swing through lightly wooded farmland and range, and again the surface is superb. A turnoff on Johnson's Siding Road just before Rapid City spits me back on Nemo Road for more frolicking on the way back to Deadwood. I had the road to myself this morning, but now I join groups of afternoon bikers enjoying the spring sun. Wow! What a great riding day.

Though the plains to the north of Deadwood and Sturgis have their own pastoral tranquility, I've discovered that the Black Hills are where South Dakota's best riding might lie: excellent engineering, smooth, swervy tarmac, cool, refreshing forests and rolling plains. No doubt about it – there *is* life in the Black Hills before Bike Week!

South Dakota
FACTS AND INFORMATION

Total Mileage

Approximately 912 miles.

In General

The Black Hills terrain of South Dakota is justly recognized as one of the nation's greatest natural assets. There, the notorious town of Deadwood has earned National Historic Landmark status, and the sterling work of Peter Norbeck, in opening up the area for travel by minimizing the impact of traffic through thoughtful and innovative highway design, deserves every motorcyclist's appreciation.

Travel Season

Weather warm enough for great riding begins in the spring. However, historically, April and May are very rainy months. Thus early to mid-summer is the best time to plan a tour in this area. Normally in June, the weather is warm and dry with plenty of sunshine, cooling off to a comfortable 50-60 degrees in the evenings.

Roads & Biking

South of Deadwood, the Black Hills offer some of the best recreational riding roads anywhere. In early June, traffic is relatively light but often jams up around Mount Rush-more, a must-see at least once in your life. To the north, there are hundreds of miles of cruising roads, and though relatively featureless, the scenery remains easy on the eyes.

The route traveled is suitable for all kinds of motorcycles and riders of almost all experience levels, although the tighter, twistier turns in the Black Hills should be treated with respect.

Maps

- *Nebraska, North Dakota and South Dakota Street Map*, Universal Maps ISBN 9780762551323, $8.95
- *South Dakota Atlas & Gazetteer* DeLorme Publishing ISBN 0899333303, $ 19.95

More Information

- Sturgis Chamber of Commerce & Visitors Bureau, www.sturgis-sd.org (605) 347-2556
- South Dakota Black Hills & Badlands www.blackhillsbadlands.com
- Historic Deadwood www.deadwood.org (800) 999-1876

Attractions

❶ Center of the Nation Monument (605) 892-2676
❷ Mount Rushmore (605) 574-2523
❸ Reptile Gardens (605) 342-5873
❹ Broken Boot Gold Mine (605) 578-1876
❺ The Mammoth Site (605) 745-6017
❻ Wind Cave National Park (605) 745-4600
❼ Black Hills Cavern, (605) 343-0542
❽ The Roo Ranch, (605) 578-1777
❾ Bear Country USA Wildlife Park (605) 343-2290

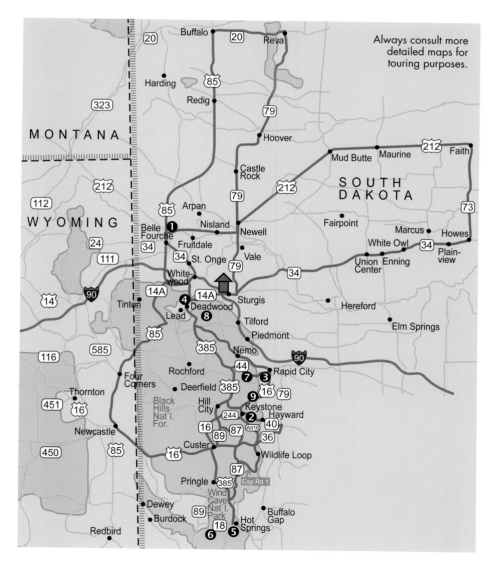

Always consult more detailed maps for touring purposes.

Southwestern Wisconsin
Two-up Tour Through Dairyland

As the miles roll on across the Southern Wisconsin countryside, it doesn't take a rocket scientist to figure out that agriculture is big around here. This fact is certainly not lost on my wife Kathy, occupying pillion. Each time the large fields of stock change, she announces it through the Air Rider communicator. To the tune of the Monty Python "Spam" song, she chants, "Corn, corn, corn..." or "Cows, cows, cows..."

↻ *Curds and curves are abundantly served in the Badger State.*

Our little singsong tribute to "America's Dairyland" has been going on for the entire tour. Oddly enough, it hasn't gotten old, nor has the scenery. Kathy sings about corn or cows, and I rock my head back and forth in unison. We surely look strange to passing motorists, but who cares? We're having a blast. The singing is as endless as is the prairie's stock of – well, you know.

Every year, Kathy and I load up the trusty Bandit and hit the road for two weeks. We choose a location, roll the dice on the weather, and hit the road. That's our idea of vacation. Those friends and family members who are not insanely jealous think we're crazy. Maybe they're right, but we always have a good time. When Christian mentioned he had a tour idea for Wisconsin, I volunteered to do it with Kathy; after all, we were going to be right there. He was reluctant to have me

work on our vacation, but I convinced him that everything would be fine. Work? Give me a break. Plus, I wanted Kathy to see first hand just what it is I'm doing all those times I ride away for days on end.

Starting in Madison, a Capital Idea

Wisconsin's state capital, Madison, is a beautiful town despite ongoing construction projects. The streets are alive with activity. An eclectic mix of hippies, skaters, and students from the University of Wisconsin weave their way through cadres of business people and legislators looking for a quick power lunch. Although Madison is certainly worth further exploration, there are lots of roads to wander. Somehow, in regards to Madison, I have a feeling that, in the words of a somewhat famous University of Wisconsin-Superior graduate, "I'll be back."

If you've never been on an extended tour, let me assure you that the best-laid plans often become moot. Despite our intentions, we find it difficult to pry ourselves from the lively streets of Madison. Yep, we get a late start. Having been on the road for over a week at this point, walking around just feels good. It's late morning before we are able to locate Route S heading west out of town. Thankfully, traffic begins to melt away as does the omnipresent road construction around the capital city. The scenery begins a transformation from commuter homes to farmland. This is the Wisconsin we're looking for.

The day is clear and beautiful. Every hilltop offers amazing views of the rolling prairie, nothing but crops and dairy pastures. For as far as the eye can see, silos dot the landscape like mushrooms after a rainstorm. The endless blue sky collides with the lush green hills in a 360-degree panorama that's a joy to behold. The bounty this land produces is nearly impossible for an average guy like me to comprehend. What's

↻ *Wisconsin's impressive capitol.*

108

not difficult for this average couple to comprehend is our own hunger. In no uncertain terms, Kathy lets me know that it's time to stop and partake.

Sauk City seems to offer some decent choices but something tells me to push on to the next town. A brisk and very enjoyable ride down sweeper-infested Route 60 lands us in Spring Green, the site of Frank Lloyd Wright's Taliesin (a Welsh word meaning "radiant brow"). Anyone interested in fine art, architecture or engineering should make the time to explore this national landmark estate (1976) located on 600 rolling acres. Arguably the greatest architect in American history, the widely ranging Wright left behind an astounding legacy of completed projects and designs; and his visionary use of materials, space, and the surrounding landscape continue to inspire architects and designers today. The town of Spring Green is obviously proud of it's most famous resident, and many of the buildings are built in the utilitarian style espoused by Mr. Wright, who began the construction of Taliesin East in 1911.

The previous week on the road has begun to take its toll. We find we're winding down earlier and earlier. It's growing late in the afternoon as we leisurely roam southward through a maze of back roads dotted with farms, woods, and streams that eventually place us on Route 78. This brings us to Route 11 and the final push of the day, to Monroe. We can go no further. There are several choices for lodging and dining. Looks like a winner.

Those Clouds Aren't That Dark, Are They?

Day two greets us with less than ideal conditions. The air is cool and the sky gray. We do our best to employ mind over matter and ignore the clouds. This tactic works well as we head north

↑ *Madison's Lake Monona as seen from Frank Lloyd Wright's Monona Terrace.*

↑ *Scooters are a popular mode of travel at the University of Wisconsin.*

↓ *We came across several of these hexagonal barns.*

on Route H. No rain here, just cows, cows, and more cows. We saw some impressive dairy farms yesterday, but the bar has been raised today. It's beginning to become all too clear why Wisconsin is known as "America's Dairyland." Thousands of curious eyes lazily follow us as we breeze down the road. I suppose two travelers on a motorcycle are just interesting enough to interrupt the cud chewing for a second or two. *Ruminating ruminants?*

The ride is chilly, but enjoyable. For some odd reason, cows fascinate Kathy and me, so we're finding this morn-

Mineral Point is actually an artsy community with a thriving downtown. Instead of grabbing a bag of peanuts next to the pumps, we linger over lunch at the Brewery Creek Brewpub. We warm up and dry out to hot coffee and hearty sandwiches. We stay at the pub as long as we can without being cited for loitering, and still the rain comes down. By the time three o'clock rolls around, the rain is not letting up and it certainly isn't getting any warmer. We declare the day a wash and make one last dash through the rain to a nearby motel. Oh well, the rest will do us good.

get away from it all. We find ourselves in Cassville on the Mississippi River in time for an early lunch. Two more fine burgers – *cows, cows, cows* – complete with hand-cut fries at the Town Pump and we're on our way. We head north on Route 133, which teases us with some nice curves but straightens out as soon as we complete the climb out of the river valley. Our arrival in Prairie du Chien lands us in traffic. There are plenty of places to stay and eat here, but the accompanying humanity holds little appeal to self-professed loners like us. Let's head on up the river.

ⓝ *Safe farming requires the proper gear.*

ⓝ *No need to hurry when the views are this nice.*

ing's ride quite fun. Things are going fine until we turn west on Route 39. It's there that the ignored clouds remind us they aren't going away. We're lucky for a while, but luck always runs out. Somewhere on Route 23, the rain begins. We lean down and make a break for Mineral Point, hoping to find a gas station awning or anything that offers shelter. To our surprise, we find much more.

"Nothing But Blue Skies Do I See..."

The rainy evening has given way to a spectacular morning. Bright blue skies and high clouds are the order of the day. We happily depart with yesterday's lousy weather behind us. We continue west on Route A, gliding across rolling hills soaking in the cool breeze. Riding in Wisconsin is relaxing and comforting, a great place to

Route 35 parallels the Mississippi and holds promise for some nice scenery. Unfortunately, it doesn't really deliver. Maybe we're expecting too much, but the river in this area looks more like a lake. There just isn't much to see and traffic is moving slowly. We're happy to reach De Soto and take that as our cue to turn inland. Here the landscape begins to change a bit. It's not as flat and there are some foothills. Sure, there are still many farms; the roads just have more zing to them. South out of Viroqua, 82 and 27 are fairly straight, but east on Route S and north again on Route 131 yields some nice riding. So nice in fact, that I lose track of time and begin to get rather stern reminders from Kathy that it's time to stop soon. I get the message and we head back to Viroqua and find a place to rest our weary bones.

One More Trip to the River

The highlighted lines on the map lead us back to the Mississippi one

form of appetizers and a beer cheese soup that is nothing short of awesome. Hunger erased and cholesterol raised, we reluctantly choose to continue on. Before we leave, we decide to check out the river one last time. The Mississippi in La Crosse is very scenic and the city celebrates this venue with a beautiful waterfront park. The area bustles with people taking in the bright, warm day. Maybe it's the knowledge that the frigid winds of winter are just around the corner, but the folks in Wisconsin seem to embrace the warm summer days with a zest few others possess.

sun. Kathy assures me that our trusty map shows Sparta being large enough to support a motel or two. As usual, she's right, and being the tour boss, she lays down the law. We stop for the evening.

How Hard Do We Ride?

Waking up to yet another spectacular Wisconsin morning, I assure Kathy that we can make it back to Madison today and finish up the tour. She looks at the map and assures me that *she's* on vacation and I may want to reconsider my estimations. Point well taken. She's right, there's no reason to push it. As with the fabulous cheeses

ᴖ *Surveying the Mississippi River in La Crosse.*

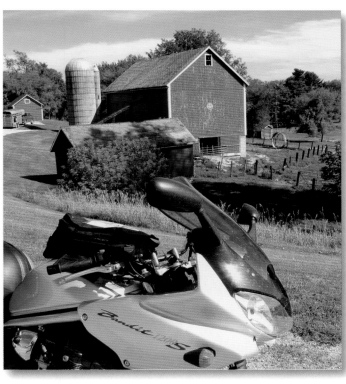

ᴖ *Family farms are everywhere in Southwestern Wisconsin.*

more time. Setting a relaxing pace, we finish up our last leg of Route 131 and head west on Route 33, bound for La Crosse. Like Madison, La Crosse has a certain energy that draws us in. We grab the first parking space we see and begin our exploration on foot. Restaurants and coffee shops abound on streets peppered with all sorts of small shops and boutiques. Lunch at Buzzard Billy's comes in the

Route 33 out of La Crosse is some of the best riding we've seen. Snaking its way east, 33 shows us elevation changes and curves that have, thus far, been eluding us. Eventually the Route 33 twist-fest morphs back into familiar, relaxing roads that ease us back into our comfortable, stress-free Wisconsin riding style. Heading north on a couple of delightful rural roads, we join up with Route 71 and head west with the

and beers of the area, these roads are to be savored, not devoured. My Speed Racer attitude readjusted, we set out to enjoy the waning days of our tour.

A long, straight Route 16 greets us as we leave Sparta. A decent road for a wake-up ride, it's uneventful yet enjoyable. Each town we roll through has some distinction to set it apart from the last and the people are friendly throughout.

◑ *Well, the price is right, but we may need a little air freshener.*

The North Carolina tags on the Bandit prompt questions wherever we stop. Our drawls are as entertaining to our northern hosts as their accents are to us. This is a really fun place to ride even if the typical Wisconsinite's idea of "down South" doesn't extend much farther than Chicago.

South on Route 33 to 58 lands us in Richland Center in time for lunch. We have many choices here, but opt for a southwestern-themed café called the Fiesta Fe. The bill is a little heftier than we're used to, but the fare is quite tasty. Recharged, we travel on.

Route 171 West to Route 61 South leads us to the banks of the Wisconsin River and Route 60 East. This road across the river bottom mixes views of the meandering river with more farms. We cross the river on Route 130 and meet up with Route 23 heading north back toward Spring Green. Unfortunately, we can't visit another architectural marvel perched on a 60-foot chimney of rock: The House on the Rock, just down the road from Taliesin. The attraction houses miles of exhibits and the world's largest carousel, but we have to take a pass. Time is not on our side this afternoon. Although we

settled on Lodi as our stop for the evening for no other reason than there should be motels there, we disagree on the pronunciation. Is it low-die or low-dee? Too tired, we forgot to ask and never found out.

Time to Go Home

We both lament the fact that it's time to start the final push to Madison and then head home. Savoring our

coffee and breakfast, we put off our departure and get an uncharacteristically late start. No worry, Madison is only a hop, skip and a jump down the road. It doesn't take long before our arrival mirrors our departure from the capital – the spacious farms slowly giving way to bedroom communities and the constancy of construction. Finally, the airport comes into sight and our Dairyland adventure ends.

The Wisconsin countryside is a very rewarding place to ride. The roads are, for the most part, in great shape considering the extreme winters. The curvy sections are just challenging enough to keep you on your toes and the straight sections allow you to relax and enjoy some marvelous scenery. Montana may be "big sky country" but let me assure you, Wisconsin's sky is pretty darn large. The rich blue sliced by emerald pastures is a contrast that never fails to impress. We loved this tour and we *will* come back. I have a sneaking suspicion that the lure of cheese curds will be too strong to keep us away for long.

◑ *A return visit to Wisconsin is a foregone conclusion.*

FACTS AND INFORMATION

Total Mileage

Approximately 837 miles.

In General

They don't call Wisconsin "America's Dairyland" for nothing – and this is farmland unlike any other. A tour here gives one a whole new appreciation for the unbelievable amount of food produced in this nation. Thankfully, most all of these farms are very well kept and provide a picture-book view of heartland America. Each ridge top offers pastoral views more amazing than the last.

Travel Season

The ideal time to ride in this area is late spring through mid-fall (May-October). Wisconsin has a reputation for varying weather conditions, although it is typically mild. Even during the prime of summer, it's not likely to get hotter than the low eighties, or to be extremely humid or rainy for any extended period.

Roads & Biking

The roads in this area of Wisconsin offer up a little of everything. The western area can throw some nice curves at you as the foothills become prominent. The smaller routes are most often named with letter designations. These roads vary in surface quality and tightness but are usually not overly challenging. Plan on getting lost, too. No matter how good a navigator you are, the roads have their own way of doing things. Getting back on track is only as far as the nearest local resident. They are friendly and know the roads are tricky.

Food & Lodging

Every town seems to have at least one restaurant, but finding accommo-dations can be a little difficult. The larger towns have ample choices, but that changes as you get out in the countryside. Some map representations make towns appear larger than they are. Do a little research on lodgings before getting caught too far out with a rapidly setting sun.

Maps

- Wisconsin AAA Map
- *Wisconsin Atlas and Gazetteer* Delorme ISBN 0899333311, $19.95

More Information

- Wisconsin Department of Tourism www.travelwisconsin.com (800) 432-8747
- Visit Madison www.visitmadison.com
- Prairie du Chien Chamber of Commerce www.prairieduchien.org

Attractions

❶ Frank Lloyd Wright's Taliesin East (608) 588-2511

❷ The House on the Rock (608) 935-3639

❸ Cave of the Mounds (608) 437-3038

❹ Cedar Grove Cheese (608) 546-5284

Always consult more detailed maps for touring purposes.

The Midwest

Southern Minnesota

River Bluffs, Prairies

Even though Minnesota lies halfway between the east and west coasts, it's not one of the dry prairie states. Millions of years ago, retreating glaciers took care of that, leaving more than 15,000 lakes behind. So, there's always water around the corner. Apart from that there is the Mississippi River Valley, cradling the state's most scenic highway, its beautiful river towns, and the exciting curves in the ravines and valleys of the bluffs in the southern region of the state.

Text: Robert Annetzberger
Photography: Robert Annetzberger and Sonja Blagojevic

AND LAKES

🎧 *Heavy metal: The Gold Wing and a Mississippi span in Red Wing.*

Day 1: Mississippi Bluffs

Dark clouds hang over Rochester and intermittent showers fall as we close in on the city. It's only 6 p.m. but it looks like midnight. Wet, tired and hungry, we finally check in at the Hampton Inn where the desk clerk says the next day's forecast calls for more of the same. Fortunately, he's wrong: The morning dawns with sunshine and blue skies all around!

In Stewartville, we turn left on Highway 30 and leave all the traffic behind us for an enjoyable ride through the countryside. East, past Chatfield, we come upon some hills and curves that make the ride on Highway 6 even more pleasurable. I could have been having so much fun on the Gold Wing that I wasn't paying attention or maybe the map wasn't accurate enough, but somehow we left 6 and got back on Highway 30. Seems we missed a turn to the right. Instead of heading for Lewiston and Winona, we're approaching Rushford. It's too late to double back;

so, we continue north on Highway 43, right across the bluffs, into southeast Minnesota, the only mountainous part of the state.

🎧 *"Good day, sunshine," in Lanesboro.*

Descending from the ridge, we eventually drive into Winona, a city of 30,000 that's enclosed on three sides by the waters of the Mississippi River. People on Harleys and others in boats seem to be having a fine time puttering about on a Sunday afternoon. "It's the first nice day after weeks of rain," the friendly lady at the visitor center says, explaining the crowds.

After circling through the sleepy city, we drive up to the scenic overlook on Garvin Heights for a spectacular view of Winona and the Mississippi. As we prepare to leave, a stranger approaches and hands us two Minnesota maps. "I think they'll do you some good," he says and then disappears. *Well, thanks, sir – what a nice surprise!*

Following Highway 17 up into the mountains offers some nice curves, and we ride eastward parallel to I-90 until descending toward the mighty river again. For a couple of miles we let it roll on, enjoying great views of the

↥ *Hwy 16 along the Root River is one of the finest roads in the region.*

From Rushford on, Highway 16 becomes even more beautiful in the Root River Valley, which seems to be the place to be for a weekend off. There are quite a few bikes on the road and lots of canoes in the water. It's late afternoon when we get to Lanesboro and slow the pace. Filled with nice examples of nineteenth-century architecture and, on this particular weekend, bicycle riders, the town is located along the 42-mile-long Root River Bike Trail.

Many people in this region come from German stock, so it almost feels

Mississippi from The Great River Road (Hwy 61), often described as one of the most scenic drives in the U.S.

Two miles past La Crescent, we turn away from the river. Staying on Scenic Highway 16, we follow the Root River through hilly farmland until we return to Rushford, a regional crossroads where bikers are coming at us from all directions. During our coffee break at the gas station, a couple on a black Gold Wing rolls up to chat. Obviously, we're not from around here, and they thank us for bringing some nice weather for a change. The woman adds, "I hope you're planning to stay awhile!"

↥ *You're often alone for miles on pure prairie pavement.*

↧ *The landscape between Faribault and Mankato is blessed with many lakes.*

like we're coming home when we step inside Lanesboro's "Das Wurst Haus" (the sausage house) where they sell their own tasty brands of German meats, sausages, bread and even root beer. A pound or two heavier, we wander on westward into the evening sun, passing by woods, and cattle nodding in the fields.

Reaching Preston, it turns out there's no way for us to make a left turn onto Highway 14. It just doesn't exist. We follow Highway 12 instead, which splits up into 12 and 14 after a few miles, and the map the stranger in Winona gave us really proves helpful. Once on Highway 14, we continue westward, reach Highway 63 again, and roll back into Rochester.

Day 2: Prairie & Lakes

Westward-ho again, to the flat part of southern Minnesota. Highway 52 takes us to Douglas and Highway 14. No mountains like yesterday, just flat farmland, and as we try to drive into Nerstrand Big Woods State Park, near Northfield, the pavement suddenly ends. Our fully loaded Gold Wing can't handle

◖ *Lake Elysian.*

◖ *Southern Minnesota countryside.*

◗ *The Whitewater Wildlife Area between Winona and Rochester.*

any of that business, so we have to find another way to Faribault, a gateway to the lakes in the southwest. That translates into 80 miles of very lonesome riding. But from Faribault on, we find plenty of company winding with us beside the beautiful lakes Minnesota is famous for. It's Memorial Day. The weather is perfect, and everyone with a boat is heading for water.

Over and over again, we take the side roads off of Highway 60 to get closer to the action on Cannon Lake,

Elysian Lake, Lake Madison…and wherever we stop to linger a great view awaits. Those who can stay longer have a great variety of camping grounds and resorts on Highway 60 to frequent.

Approaching Mankato from the east on Highway 14, we turn northward on Highway 27. I can't resist following the "public access" sign to Lake Washington, and once there on the shoreline we realize it was definitely worth that extra mile. Boats skim the water in all directions and quite a few Harleys are parked in front of the lakeside café. Unfortunately, with so much traveling left in the day, we can't join the other riders relaxing on the terrace.

for Austin and I-90. Highway 63 gets us back to Rochester. All totalled, it's three hundred, semi-exhausting miles.

Day 3: Along the Mississippi

The Midwest heat continues to broil us as we leave Rochester and roam northward on our third leg of the trip. Fifty miles up Highways 52 and 58, we arrive in Red Wing on the Mississippi. Hundreds of baskets overflowing with flowers hang from the lamp posts to brighten the streets and historic storefronts. As seen from above, in Memorial Park, it's even prettier, more impressive. And the scenic highlights just keep coming from the many overlooks we stop at heading south along The Great River Road.

the river valley around Minnesota City to run through a nice curvy stretch into the mountains on Hwy 284. It's a blessing after so many straight-shot miles the day before.

There are more good curves in the Whitewater Wildlife Area north of Elba. Pure, unadulterated nature. A village named Beaver used to be here, but the site was vacated decades ago. Just about the only sign left that the area was ever inhabited is the overgrown cemetery.

In Millville, we hit Highway 11 and all of a sudden it's clear we've found the perfect road to end our roundtrip. Winding along 11 through the Zumbro River Valley for about ten miles, it's a

⋂ *A steep, curving road rewards us with this view of Red Wing and the river in Memorial Park.*

Much of the afternoon is taken up in the green monotony of corn rows and the moo-mentous features of dairy country. The sun bears down on miles of flat sameness, and we get the feeling we're little more than pieces moving over a board game. The winners are the ones who manage to keep their eyes open.

Crossing I-35, we reach Blooming Prairie, head for Hayfield, and turn south

At Lake City, we pause awhile in the public park next to the marina for another spectacular view of Lake Pepin. A little known factoid: the sport of waterskiing was invented here in 1922 by a guy named Ralph Samuelson. Now that must have been a sight!

Wabasha, dating back to the 1830s, is one of Minnesota's oldest towns and home to the National Eagle Center. Shortly before we reach Winona again, we leave

lot of fun steering the big Honda through the curves – and although this route may not be as well known as the one we rode two days ago between Rushford and Preston, it's just as scenic, and the curves are definitely better. Refreshing!

While saying our goodbyes the next day, the dark clouds return to see us off. We didn't care a bit though, after three perfectly bright days in multifaceted Minnesota.

FACTS AND INFORMATION

Total Mileage

Approximately 622 miles.

In General

Southern Minnesota offers a mixture of flat prairie and farmland, mountains in the southeast and, of course, beautiful towns like Red Wing, Lake City, and Winona along the Mississippi River. Glaciers shaped Minnesota, raking most of the land completely flat; but in retreat, they left more than 15,000 lakes in their wake. Today, 95 percent of the state's population lives within ten minutes of a body of water. Rochester, our headquarters for the trip, has often been described as "the most livable city" in the U.S.

Travel Season

Due to Minnesota's cold climate, the riding season is shorter than many may like. It's still a little chilly during the spring, even in May. Thus, the best time for touring this area is mid to late summer. July and August are generally the warmest and driest months for traveling.

Roads & Biking

Generally, the roads are in very good condition. Byways over the prairie and farmland are usually flat and straight, but Bluff Country in the southeast offers lots of mountains and curves. Scenic Highway 61 (The Great River Road) along the Mississippi is definitely the most spectacular. Hwy 16 from Rushford to Preston is also recommended for its beauty, along with Highway 60 (between Faribault and Mankato) for touring Minnesota lake country.

Food & Lodging

A good choice of motels and restaurants can be found along the route. One notable restaurant worth visiting in Lanesboro is The Wurst Haus, serving homemade German food and craft beer.

Maps

o Official Minnesota Highway Map Minnesota Department of Transportation

More Information

o Red Wing Visitors & Convention Bureau (800) 498-3444 www.redwing.org

o Winona Convention & Visitors Bureau (800) 657-4972 www.visitwinona.com

o Rochester Convention & Visitors Bureau www.rochestercvb.org

o Explore Minnesota, (651) 296-5029 www.exploreminnesota.com

o Minnesota Dept. of Transportation www.dot.state.mn.us

Attractions

❶ Nerstrand Big Woods State Park (507) 333-4840

❷ National Eagle Center (651) 565-4989

❸ Historic Pickwick Mill (507) 457-0499

❹ Forestville/Mystery Cave State Park (507) 352-5111, (507) 937-3251

❺ Quarry Hill Nature Center (507) 281-6114

❻ Mayowood Mansion (507) 282-9447

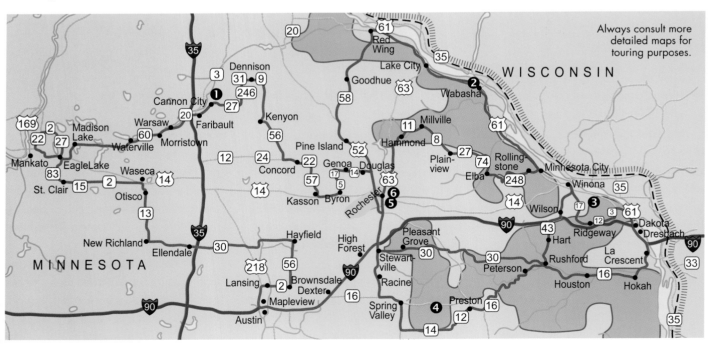

The Dark Side

A gas tank miscalculation means I'm riding through the Gifford-Pinchot National Forest after dark. Dense evergreens crowd the road, filtering out any moonlight that might have squeezed through the clouds, and the dark tarmac seems to drain the brightness from my headlight. As I round a right-hander, the dappled rear end of a deer, as high as my windshield, appears in my headlight beam no more than six feet ahead. In an instant it's gone.

How I failed to make contact, I'll never know. In daylight or even dusk, I would have seen the deer easily. This time, at night, under an obscuring canopy of trees... I guess I just got lucky. We need to consider two important aspects of riding at night – seeing and being seen – and take the necessary action to mitigate potential disaster.

Seeing

Arguably, I might have seen my Gifford-Pinchot deer much sooner if my bike had been fitted with accessory lights. Stock motorcycle lighting was pretty ineffective until the latest crop of projector headlights arrived. First, motorcycle headlights (assuming you have more than one) have to be close together, simply because we're talking about a single-track vehicle, so that they don't have the same beam spread as a car's broader-spaced headlights.

Second, motorcycle headlights are often badly adjusted to start with and sometimes difficult to adjust right. Adding or removing luggage will also upset your headlight settings, though some touring bikes now incorporate a remote headlight adjuster.

So, what can you do to improve your lighting? Accessory lights are certainly an option, and there are plenty of well-known manufacturers of excellent accessory lights and fittings, such as PIAA, Pro-One, Lockhart-Phillips, etc. Just make sure your bike's electrical system can cope, especially if you're using other high-current accessories, like heated clothing.

You also need to consider the type of lights you're adding: Though high-intensity projector lights will cut through a clear, dark night, they are basically useless in fog because the water droplets scatter light. Amber fog lights with a broad beam will work much better in these conditions. Another option is to upgrade your existing headlights.

Regardless of how much light power you have, you should never ride so fast that your stopping distance is greater than the distance you can see. Be especially careful of this when passing a slower car. Cars usually have better lighting, and in accelerating to pass, you may find you're going too fast for your sight distance.

Being Seen

Many riders eschew them, but hi-vis vests work. The Hurt Report concluded that involvement in collisions was "significantly reduced" for riders wearing high-visibility clothing. My vest cost $16.95 from an industrial safety supplier, and I doubt there's any better "conspicuity" bang for the buck.

But if riding around looking like a highway maintenance worker offends your fashion sense, what are some other options? Having reflective areas on your motorcycle wear will certainly help, and though most purpose-made bike clothing already includes patches made from materials such as 3M Scotchlite®, it doesn't hurt to add more. Reflective patches and tape are available from www.ridesafer.com.

As far as your bike is concerned, you can increase its visibility either passively or actively. The passive route calls for reflectors. Or you can take the active approach and fit accessory lights to your bike that increase its visibility at night.

A number of companies can offer ways of increasing your bike's night visibility. Kisan Technologies Vectra-Light is a neat LED turn-signal array that fits to your wing mirrors and lights each LED sequentially so that there's no doubt left in a dumb driver's mind which way you're turning. And if you've ever realized the reason a car turned in front of you was because your turn signal was left on, Kisan also offers a Signal Minder kit, which automatically cancels turn signals. The Signal Minder can also be set to operate your turn signals as running lights or four-way flashers. Both of these items are available from www.sporttouringusa.com, which also sells its own 16 red LED Hyper-Lite array that illuminates to warn drivers you're slowing down or stopping.

Is Your Journey Necessary?

There's no question, all other things being equal, that riding a motorcycle at night is more dangerous than riding during the day. It's sometimes worth asking the question: Why do it? There always seems to be more to consider on the risk side of that risk/reward ledger once the sun has gone down. So, is an exciting ride at night worth taking the extra risk? That's a decision only you can make.

Eastern Ohio
Rolling Hills Road Trip

Text & Photography: Chris Myers

Why did the black snake cross the road? I don't know either. Maybe he's fleeing to higher ground from the floodwaters that have recently plagued the Eastern Ohio countryside. Maybe the critters on his menu are just a bit more succulent on the other side. Either way, he doesn't have far to go to reach safety. Traffic is light and the day is beautiful. Mr. Blacksnake need not be concerned with the speedy wheels of a certain Aprilia Falco. The Falco is hunting all right, but with bigger snakes in mind. Its prey has been found and we're bearing down on the twisting, undulating, serpentine beast known as the Eastern Ohio back road.

Like the black snake, Ohio's country lanes are peaceful and somewhat benign. On the other hand, if approached too aggressively, they'll usually reward you with a painful bite. This is not an indictment against said roads, quite the opposite in fact. As riders, we look for challenging roads. We like to flick our machines back and forth, leaning into turns, braking in, accelerating out, up and down hills, and all the while

123

↻ *Ohio has plenty of curves, you just have to know where to look.*

catching glimpses of the landscape unfolding beneath us as we fly by. Most riders have a certain appreciation for living on the edge and these Ohio side roads certainly have plenty of edge to offer them.

↻ *Sunny days are happy days.*

Getting There is Half the Fun, They Say

Riding in Ohio will be a new experience. With the one exception of a jaunt taken along the Ohio River several years ago, I am in uncharted territory. The ride across West Virginia was fantastic, as usual, and I'm primed to make Canton in time to find a room and search for a nice hot meal. Interstate 77 is boring but reasonably scenic, and the earlier cloudiness has given way to a bright, sunny afternoon.

How quickly Mother Nature throws her meteorologic wrench in my gearbox. In what seems a matter of minutes, the sky turns an ominous shade of inky gray..."the weather started getting rough, the tiny bike was tossed, if not for the courage of the fearless dude, the Falco would be lost, the Falco would be lost..." [Sorry, one too many episodes of "Gilligan's Island" as a kid.] Honestly though, by the time I find an exit I'm beginning to feel a bit like Gilligan and the Skipper in the gale that always opens that "classic" sitcom.

I seek refuge in a small diner and start in on the decaf, wondering if it always rains sideways in Ohio. Not the auspicious welcome I was hoping for. *Come on Ohio, work with me here, I'm the new guy.* I later find out there were reports of at least one tornado touching down several miles away. A waterlogged couple riding what appears in the rain to be a very pretty Springer Softail come in saying they had to ride down off the road because the lightning was just too close for comfort. Eventually, the rain begins to just look like rain, as opposed to some kind of satanic car wash, and that's my cue to leave. But a short ride through the still heavy precipitation is more than enough for this kid. As far as I'm concerned, the yellow sign of the Super 8 motel reads Waldorf-Astoria. And to think, this tour hasn't even started.

What a difference a night makes. The Saturday morning sunshine shoots through the opened curtains with an intensity that slams my pupils shut so fast I'm seeing only spots. Fully expecting cloudiness at best, the brilliant blue sky is indeed a welcome, if startling sight. My timing seems to be perfect. I'm told the weather has been terrible in the area up to this point. Luckily, the motorcycle gods are smiling upon me and the weather will not be a *direct* issue for the rest of the tour. But more on that later. It's time to hit the road.

A Horse is a Horse, of Course, of Course...

A nice morning ride to Canton gets day one going and the riding juices flowing. I'd love to see the Pro Football Hall of Fame, but the possibility of encountering a huge weekend crowd scares me away. Maybe next time – Thorpe, Hallas, Staubach and all of the other gridiron heroes of days past will have to wait. The roads I'm riding in Canton are in terrible shape. The city seems to have a nice downtown area, but the ride in is more suited to a dual sport than a sport tourer: *Sorry Canton, I'm outta here.*

♬ *Traveling in Ohio sure has come a long way.*

Route 800 south is a fairly nice road but fails to offer much in the way of scenery. Damage from the severe storms is evident along the route. Creeks and rivers are running very high and resemble roiling cauldrons of poorly made cappuccino seasoned with a generous helping of flotsam and jetsam. A quick stop at the Zoar Village State Memorial is a nice break. The village was originally a settlement of German religious dissenters called the Society of Separatists of Zoar. The Old World architecture has been restored and there are many displays depicting the life and times of the Zoarists in the early 1800s. It's a neat place to explore.

On down Route 800, one finds New Philadelphia, a pretty town with more than enough options for food and lodging. Unfortunately, it's too early for lunch, so I press on for Route 39, heading west from New Philadelphia into the heart of the Ohio Amish country. I'm looking forward to seeing the simple expressions of Amish culture in the Sugar Creek and Walnut Creek areas. Apparently so are several zillion other

folks. Sugar Creek looks like a traveling tour bus rodeo performing a promotional gig in the parking lot of an RV dealership. If an object can even remotely be associated with the Amish, I'm sure somebody is selling it there. And since shopping is not my thing, I'm ready to go. This tourism is great for the area; I just prefer to use the motorcycle to escape the rat race, not compete in it. And if any of you understand the feeling, don't make the mistake of traveling in these parts on a weekend.

There are obviously many places to find food and, as best I can tell, lodging in Sugar Creek and nearby in Walnut Creek. Route 39 is like Route 800 in the sense that it's a pretty ride, but the road is somewhat unexciting. I'm beginning to think that this part of Ohio may be devoid of interesting roads. But today's roads, like yesterday's weather, are about to change, and fast. After another game of minivan dodgeball in Walnut Creek, I'm ready to get some air. A left on Route 557 gets me out of traffic quite nicely, thank you, and that's when I begin to see what the area is really all about.

🎧 *A grand mural in tribute to the steel industry in Steubenville.*

Farms and open land abound on the narrow winding road. This is getting interesting. Routes 557, 643 and Route 83 are all fun roads with plenty of scenery and curves to keep you busy. However, if you do find yourself thinking about scampering over the roads in this area, be aware of the Amish buggies. They are easy to see and they're kept well to the right of the road, but they are horse-drawn. I quickly found that it's not a bad idea to keep toward the centerline and to stay most attentive when cresting hills and going through blind corners. The horses' exhaust systems also leave telltale signs in the road. I try to avoid the "apples," they can't be good for traction. Damage and injury aside, imagine having to explain that one to your riding buddies.

It's lunchtime and I find myself in Millersburg. A quick bite to eat and some peaceful moments of air-conditioned repose and I'm on my way again. Just outside of Butler, I make a wrong turn onto Wheatcraft Road, which turns into another one of those back-road happy accidents. This "mistake" happens to be a great little asphalt rollercoaster ride through the country. I'm totally lost but get back on track in Mount Vernon. The day is drawing to a close, though it's not over yet. Routes 205, 514 and 520 are a blast and allow my head to ignore the gathering complaints from my wrists and seat. My original goal of Coshocton is nixed, too, when a fellow rider informs me that Route 60 is flooded. Mother Nature strikes again. Oh well, revert to Plan B: Back to Millersburg and a room for the night.

Take Me to the River

Sunday morning is bright, and day two promises to be a hot one. A quick ride down to Coshocton and another neat place to stop: Historic Roscoe Village, a restored Ohio and Erie Canal town. The canal was constructed in the early 1800s to transport people and goods from ports on the Ohio River and Lake Erie throughout Ohio. Today, craftsmen reproduce articles from the era and there are horse-drawn canal boats that show folks what transportation way back when was like. Route 83 south is perfect for a morning ride, scenic and not too challenging, a nice wake-up ride. Yes, I'm awake, and it's a good thing as I turn onto Route 658. This road is narrow, twisty and tight, and ends in a river. Well, today it did. I kid you not. Again, the weather foils the best-laid plans. The road is underwater so I must retreat – *c'est la vie.*

Creative map work and a little luck soon have me back on track and heading for Uhrichsville. The Village of Gnadenhutten is on the way and proves to be another good rest stop. Quiet, off the main road, this historic site on the Tuscarawas River offers shade and picnic tables to the weary traveler. Routes 800 and 799 present a nice relaxing ride through the country and my favorite lunch option, the roadside drive-in. You know the place – order from a walk-up window and eat at a picnic table. I love gourmet food, but honestly, I'll take a hot dog served in foil and a cold soda any time. The views of Clendening Lake from Route 799 are nice and make it worth keeping an eye out for this road if you're in the area.

Starting in Cadiz and heading north, the ride really opens up. Wow, these are some fantastic roads. Hit these babies on a weekday when traffic is light and you *will* have fun, I promise. The route on your pullout tank bag map all the way to Steubenville is great, featuring every type of road imaginable. Some are a little more crowded than others, but all are fun. The highlight here is the section of Route 151

from Jewett to Steubenville. The beauty of the endless rolling hills has an almost hypnotic effect as you ride the ridge tops approaching the Ohio River. When these slopes and valleys melt into the twilit sky, it's a sight to behold. The riding has been spectacular today, but I've had enough. I'm tired, hungry, but confident that Steubenville will come through and provide "whiskey for my men and beer for my horses."

In Search of Dino Crocetti

The wine and pizza did the trick: I slept like a baby. My last day on the road in Ohio. I better get moving. Steubenville is known as the 'city of murals.' All over town, the sides of buildings are painted with big, bright murals – 25 of them to be exact. They're everywhere it seems. All of them depict scenes from Steubenville's history as a river town and industrial center, and I have been assured there is one mural dedicated to the town's most famous celebrity, Dino Crocetti. Born and raised in Steubenville, he left home at 17 to make it big in show business. No one can deny that the man the world came to know as Dean Martin did OK for himself. But for me, finding his

↺ *Scalp intact, General George A. Custer stands watch over his birthplace in New Rumley.*

ᑎ *The black snake did more than cross the road, he inspired its design.*

mural proves more elusive than the fame he sought. I get lost trying to find it.

Unfortunately, my time does not allow a more thorough exploration of Steubenville. I have the impression this city, like many others on the river, has seen better days; yet, there is an underlying sense that despite tough times, the city will adapt and overcome. There is a rich history here, and I'd like to get back some day and dig deeper. But, again, the road beckons. *So long Steubenville, thanks for the great pizza!*

Route 213 is a steep climb out of the Ohio River Valley, and it's too bad that thick underbrush and tall stands of hardwoods prohibit any chance of getting a bird's-eye view of the river. The road is good but populated. Exercise caution here, as there are many

driveways and businesses. Eventually, it gets more fun as the city slips away. Be careful or you'll miss the turn toward Ironton, I did. This one ends in Monroeville and it's a hoot. Very narrow and undulating, it gives the impression I'm saddled to a bronco, not a well-mannered sport bike. My goofy grin was probably evident as I pulled into Salineville. A word of warning, though: gas stations in this area are hard to find. The few I did see are out of business. If it gets really bad, stop and ask – the folks in Ohio are very friendly and more than happy to point you in the right direction. My reserve light had been on far too long for comfort as I roll in to Minerva, another town good for a stop. Route 43 leads the intrepid Falco south toward Atwood Lake. A stiff breeze has kicked up the whitecaps and taken the edge

off of an otherwise hot day. These are the days we live for as riders.

Heading north again, I begin to see signs for Canton. My Ohio adventure is ending. As the miles to my final destination of the tour dwindle to single digits, I reflect upon the past three days. Initially, I did not know what to expect riding in Eastern Ohio. I was influenced by stereotypical visions of the "Midwest" as this huge stretch of flats that's only good for farming and occupying the space between mountain ranges. How wrong I was. I found some truly inspiring roads. And the rolling hills, lakes, rivers and farmland supplied a memory bank full of great scenery. The riding was just plain fun.

So, would I go to Ohio to ride again? You bet I would. ᑐ

FACTS AND INFORMATION

Total Mileage

Approximately 556 miles.

In General

Eastern Ohio runs the gamut from crowded tourist areas to places where you may not see a car for 30 minutes or more, especially in Amish country. They live and work here and, of course, their mode and manner of transportation is quite different from ours. They keep their horse-drawn buggies to the right, and sharing the road shouldn't pose problems for attentive riders. Passing slowly, at lowered rpm to keep the horse from spooking, is the proper etiquette.

Many historic sites dot Eastern Ohio. Some are little more than roadside markers, and others are lovingly restored communities. Zoar Village State Memorial and Roscoe Village are vivid reminders of the past.

Travel Season

The best time to travel this area is spring. The upper-80 temperatures experienced during this tour are unusual for late May. Average highs range from 63 in April to 84 in July, falling to 65 in October. Severe weather is quite capable of rearing its ugly head in late May, and carrying rain gear is advisable.

Roads & Biking

Don't let the rolling hills and easygoing nature of the landscape fool you. There are some serious twisties here. The roads are, for the most part, in very good shape; but you should be prepared to adapt without much notice. Some routes deteriorate suddenly, and many of the smaller ones are very tricky. The surfaces are center crowned which makes for off-camber situations in almost every turn.

Maps

- *Rand McNally Folded Map: Ohio*
  Rand McNally & Company
  ISBN 052899476X, $4.95
- *AAA Ohio State Road Map*

More Information

- Discover Ohio
  www.discoverohio.com
- Amish Country Ohio
  (877) 643-8824
  www.visitamishcountry.com

Attractions

❶ Historic Roscoe Village
  (740) 622-9310
❷ Zoar Village, (330) 874-4336
❸ The Alpaca Rosa
  (330) 699-2182
❹ Historic Fort Steuben
  (740) 283-1787
❺ Gospel Hill Lighthouse
  (740) 824-3300

The Midwest

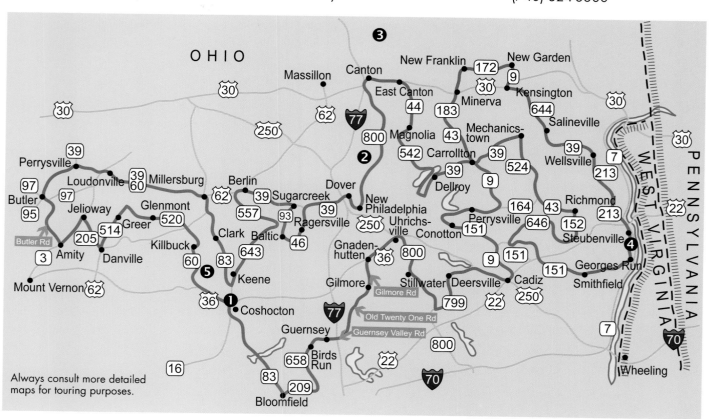

Always consult more detailed maps for touring purposes.

The Southeast

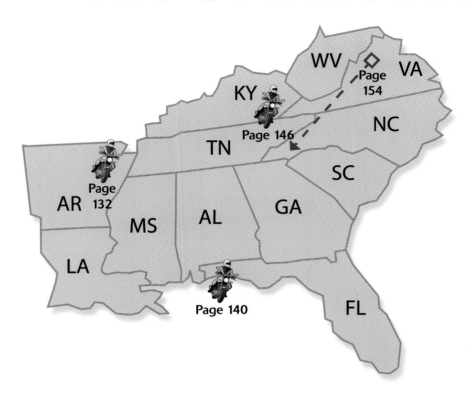

Colliding tectonic plates thrust the Appalachian Mountains skyward some 300 to 600 million years ago, according to geologists. These mountains rose to heights rivaling peaks in the modern-day Rocky Mountains, but eons of erosion wore them down to the green, gently rounded mountain ridges seen today. The Appalachian Mountains largely define the topography, history and scenic beauty of the Southeast.

The Southeast also has a vibrant history for visitors to discover, from Virginia's restored Colonial Williamsburg settlement to the many preserved Civil War battlefields and museums scattered throughout the southeastern states. Mild winters and warm, humid summers are the usual weather patterns here, which makes for a longer touring season.

The Southeast has some of the best scenic touring routes in all of the US: Tennessee's US 129; the Blue Ridge Parkway, tracking high above the beautiful Shenandoah Valley, in Virginia and North Carolina; the Cherohala Skyway in Tennessee; the many twisty roads in eastern Kentucky; Arkansas's Route 7; The Natchez Trace Parkway and the dramatic vistas along two-lane tarmac in "Wild and Wonderful" West Virginia. This is going to be fun, so hold on tight!

EASTERN ARKANSAS
THE LONG AND UNWOUND ROAD

The light slanting through the slit in the blackout curtains seems to indicate the day has dawned bright and sunny. Slowly, like a tortoise, my dream-fogged head extrudes from the dark shell of the motel room at the door and swivels in the outside world. Yes, it's a beautiful morning to begin a tour. A familiar grin tugs on the corners of my mouth and suddenly I'm ready for that first cup of bad coffee.

Text and Photography: Chris Myers

Don't get me wrong – I love a *good* cup of joe. But there's just something about a watery, cardboard, lifeless splash of tannic swill that lets you know you're really on the road. Teaming up with the first breeze of fresh morning air, I'm ready to move on, to a better cup of coffee if nothing else. The "free" coffee at the same Interstate-accessible stack-o-racks that welcomed this weary traveler last night is shooing me away today. I know Little Rock has good brew somewhere, but the need to explore has me defying Captain Caffeine's orders to discover a proper mug. In this southern town, said mug found too often would then lead me on to biscuits, gravy, sausage, and eggs, and I certainly don't have time for a nap just yet.

Thrice the Rice

Gold Wing gassed and ready to roll, I bid the Arkansas capital adieu and watch the city fade into the horizon in the rearview. There's nothing wrong with cities, but I always find when riding that they look much better going than coming, unless it's late and I'm looking for a room. I race with the warm morning breeze, heading east across long straight country roads into the agricultural heart of the Natural State. The eastern Arkansas Delta region is nearly tabletop flat and the Wing easily gobbles the miles of Route 38 toward Des Arc.

🜂 *Future rice paddies await spring flooding.*

The size of the fields is nearly incomprehensible. The distant tractors are small, slow-moving points trailing

🜂 *I'll take the blue one, please.*

expanding, windblown billows of dust. The big diesels break and furrow the rich alluvial soil deposited over millions of years by the flooding of the Mississippi River and its many tributaries. It's a deep, ancient sediment that nourished thriving communities long before the first European explorer, Hernando De Soto, arrived in 1541.

Over my years of traveling throughout the countryside, I've developed a pretty decent sense of which crops are which. Around these parts though, I find myself a bit confused about what these farmers are up to. It's spring and the planting hasn't been done yet, so I'm left to deduce the intended harvest by the way the fields are being prepared. These huge, flat fields are crisscrossed with serpentine, knee-high lines of soil, and despite the seemingly random placement of these graceful earthworks, there seems to be a method to the madness. After miles of curious musings, my amateur agrarian sleuthing finally puts

↻ *If I had to guess, I'd say they're full of rice.*

two and two together when permanent water pumps become part of the mix. These super-sized spigots are obviously designed to flood the areas contained within these alluvial levees creating – rice paddies. Okay, maybe those signs for the Arkansas rice farmers cooperatives helped a little, but I figured it out, by golly. I later read that Arkansas is the nation's leading rice-producing state, accounting for nearly one-fifth of the total U.S. crop. So, if you ever learn you have a long lost Uncle Ben in Arkansas, be nice to him.

My eastern trek turns in a northwesterly direction in Des Arc with a left on Route 11. Although the roads are still long and straight, there seems to be a bit of a change afoot as I near Searcy. The flat expanses slowly begin to give way to rolling hills. The Delta scenery isn't bad, but miles and miles of flat fields do become a bit tame after a while. The sheer size of the farms and the amount of food they must produce is amazing, but to roving motorcyclists – well, we find more inspiration when plowing through the curves and swoops.

↻ *Somewhere in that swamp, the Ivory-Billed Woodpecker still flies.*

135

It's nearing lunchtime as I approach Batesville. My golf nut dad claims he can "smell" driving ranges when he's on the road. I know the feeling, but with me it's barbecue joints, and I have a hunch I'm not too far from one about the time my belly puts my eyes and nose on alert. I pass by the Batesville Speedway, a 3/8-mile dirt track that has to be one of Batesville native and NASCAR star Mark Martin's former haunts. If there's a racetrack, there's got to be some good "bad for you" food nearby. Sure enough, not too far up the road, I find just the spot. Dad's sixth sense nets him a bucket of golf balls, mine a plate of tender pork. I leave it to you: Whose mutant power would you rather have?

Back on the road and reenergized, I guide the Wing in the direction of Batesville proper and shoot the short but steep and curvy descent into the White River Valley. Here, in the foothills of the Ozark Mountains, there are plenty of places to find a bite, and a room shouldn't be a problem either. The historic downtown of Batesville drips with southern ambiance and looks like it would be fun to explore. Unfortunately, an ominous and suddenly cool breeze riding in on some low slate-colored clouds decides it in favor of a quick getaway. Thankfully, the ugly skies are more rumble than rain and I'm able to make it to Pocahontas with only a few drops on the windshield to show for it. As I'm checking in at the Days Inn, I can't help but think how nice it would be if they had..."a hot tub down by the pool," the medium moonlighting as a desk clerk informs me. She can uncouple my train of thought any time. Ah, the benefits of coming in off the road a bit early – there's plenty of time to have a soak and watch the clouds roll in.

Delta Rising

The city of Pocahontas bills itself "Where the Delta Rises to Meet the Ozarks." Despite more unfriendly clouds, I choose to hit the road. Eh, they're high clouds, I reason. Pulling out of the Days Inn parking lot, I look east and see an eternal flatness. The tour route has me headed northwest on Route 90 and soon I'm rolling up through the Ozark foothills. I can't argue against the accuracy of the city's claim.

About the time I enter Missouri for a short stint in the Show Me State, the foreboding skies have given way to a sparkling clarity punctuated by a few wisps of cottony clouds. The warm breeze is back and the dancing spring grasses seem to burst forth in a gathering greenness that takes on a most unnatural shade of emerald. Days like these, my friends, are why we ride. Somewhere in this euphoric haze of nature finally letting go of winter, I miss a turn and get lost. Darn the luck, now I have to explore. After a healthy dose of country tranquility, I find my way back to the route and continue on, back toward Pocahontas.

East on Route 304, the Delta has taken over again. Straight roads and huge farms dominate the scenery. Then from nowhere, a hill appears and the road regains some personality. Winding my way up from the farmland, I find myself atop Crowley's Ridge. This unusual geographic phenomena, named for Benjamin Crowley, one of the first settlers to reach the area, rises from the perfectly horizontal horizons of the surrounding alluvial plain and stretches nearly 200 miles north to south from just below Cape Girardeau, MO, to Helena, AR. It's thought that Crowley's Ridge once stood as an island of sorts between the ancient courses of the Ohio and Mississippi Rivers. As the riverbeds changed over the eons, the exposed land was left standing, surrounded by the flat delta. Loess, or windblown soil, accumulated over the years creating elevations from 250 to over 500 feet on the ridge that's anywhere from three to twelve miles across.

Crowley's namesake has become the home to many of the area's cities and towns due to its natural protection from floods. And let's face it, where you have elevation changes, you generally

136

have good riding. Crowley's Ridge is no exception. A short stretch of Route 168 north of Jonesboro gives me a taste of what this interesting area's roads are like, but then the tour veers back into the Delta. With the sun beginning its daily osmosis from bright yellow to a burnt western orange, I can't decide if my tired eyes are the result of a visit from the sandman or irritation from the alluvial grit riding along on the ubiquitous prairie breeze. Either way, the map indicates that Newport is probably my best choice for finding a bed for the evening.

To the Ridge and Back

After spending several minutes gulping down the cool morning air, I rejoin the chase. The scenery is composed of another stretch of farms and linear roads until the route eventually winds its way back to Crowley's Ridge. Once out of the Delta I pick up Route 163, appropriately called Crowley's Ridge Parkway, near Harrisburg. From there, the ride south to Madison is a much needed distraction from the preceding flatness. The Ridge is home to many different varieties of flora and "twistae"

↻ *See, not every road in Eastern Arkansas is flat and straight.*

I know where I am… I think.

not found anywhere else in the area. The sights and rounds are pleasant, working both the senses and the steering. Unfortunately, all good things must come to an end and the route dives back into the Delta flats. Heading west on Route 306, the series of roads leading to the White River are impressive again in their curve-free lengths as well as the boundless acreage devoted to food production. I'll never look at a box of Minute Rice the same way again.

While my descriptions may have you thinking the land is drab and feature-less, that's actually not the case. Sure, there are miles of perfectly flat fields, but they're interspersed with slow swampy rivers that offer exceptional scenery. The dark, motionless water seems to foster endless varieties of plant and animal life, and the traffic on some of these roads is so light that the critters don't seem to know how to react when someone actually stops to check them out. In fact, somewhere in this area an Ivory-Billed Woodpecker, long thought extinct, was spotted alive and well. The loneliness of these roads is most assuredly

nothing compared to the vast swamps, but without chest waders and a snake-bite kit, I believe I'll leave the Ivory-Billed Woodpecker to its own devices and push on. South through DeValls Bluff, the lines on the map again get real straight. The map is accurate. I while away the last couple of hours listening to the Gold Wing's stereo and wondering what it's like to have your nearest neighbor's proximity measured in miles.

"Show me the Mizzou."

As Little Rock gets closer and closer, so does the distance between the houses. Eventually, the outskirts of the city take on a homogeneity common across the nation. Passing by neighborhoods that could be plopped into any suburban area in the country without raising an eyebrow, I can't help but wonder just how "feature-less" the landscape of the past few days has been. Living in a bedroom community myself, I see my house a hundred times over nearing the city. Are vast fields of rich soil really that dull? I, for one, found them fascinating. That's a lot more than I can say about the crops of generic homes that rise unabated in once fertile fields near the highways.

I have a long ride back to North Carolina and these visions of wide-open "featureless" land will remain with me for a long time to come. And when I get to my little section of I-40, I'll peel off at my exit and make the brief final leg of my journey through yet another unremarkable plot of brick and vinyl houses that could fit in nearly any neighborhood in the country. But I don't care so much about that. It's home, and I know the coffee is incredible.

FACTS AND INFORMATION

Total Mileage

Approximately 751 miles.

In General

Travelers are first struck by the enormous scope of the fertile Mississippi Delta in this region of Arkansas, although the landscape's features are somewhat unremarkable. Fortunately, the flat ride is interlaced with welcome, winding breaks on roads meandering across the Ozark foothills and Crowley's Ridge.

Travel Season

This area is best traveled in the autumn or spring when the landscape is most colorful and the days are warm and sunny. Eastern Arkansas has a milder climate than other parts of the state, but many people will still find it uncomfortably hot and muggy during the summer months.

Roads & Biking

The roads are in great condition, with very few potholes or other imperfections to worry about. Of primary concern are those places where the loose sandy soil from the fields blows onto the road. Don't let the long, straight nature of the roads lure you into a false sense of security either; there are creatures running about and an occasional sharp turn pops up out of nowhere.

Food & Lodging

Finding food is never a problem. Nearly every small town has some sort of mom 'n' pop joint to feed the farmers, and the portions are good and hearty. The bigger towns have the usual fast food and franchise rows for the less adventurous.

When locating lodgings, take care not to stray too far from the bigger dots on the map when you find the sun making a quick getaway.

Maps

- AAA - Arkansas State Road Map
- *State Highway Tourist Map* Arkansas State Highway and Transportation Department www.arkansashighways.com
- *Arkansas Atlas & Gazetteer* Delorme Publishing ISBN 0899333451, $19.95

More Information

- Crowley's Ridge State Park (870) 573-6751
- The State Parks of Arkansas - The Natural State www.arkansasstateparks.com
- Arkansas Delta Byways www.deltabyways.com
- Arkansas Department of Parks and Tourism www.arkansas.com

Attractions

❶ The Old Mill, (501) 791-8537
❷ Old State House Museum (501) 324.9685
❸ MacArthur Museum of Arkansas Military History, (501) 376-4602
❹ Governor's Mansion (501) 324-9805
❺ Big Dam Bridge (501) 340-6800
❻ Parkin Archeological State Park (870) 755-2676

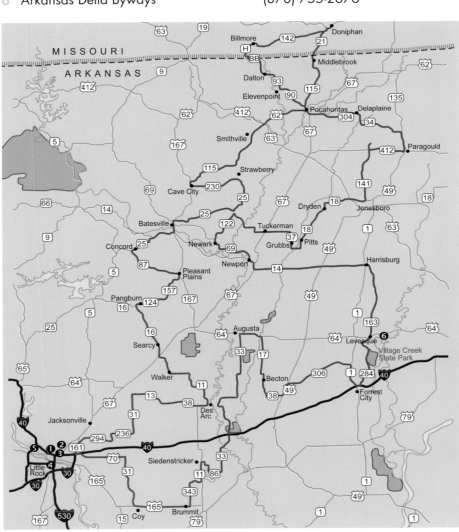

Florida Panhandle Tour
A Midwinter Shell Game

Text and Photography: Chris Myers

The R rule is one of the seafood basics I remember from my younger days on the Chesapeake Bay. If a month contains the letter R, it's OK to eat oysters. My destination is the Florida Panhandle, the month is February, and the Apalachicola area of the Panhandle happens to be world renowned for its oysters. I'm certainly no rocket scientist – they're all over at Cape Canaveral – but it appears that somebody's going to be slamming down some bivalves.

I Can't Help My Shellfishness

According to the rule, February should be the best time to chisel my way through a pail of shells. After all, it's the only month with two R's, whether the first one is pronounced or not. R regardless, the Kawasaki Concours is tossing back the southbound miles on Route 319 with ease and the prospect of hitting Tallahassee at lunchtime has me thinking college-town chow. Aside from being the Sunshine State's capital, Tallahassee is home to Florida State University. With plenty of hungry Seminoles constantly on the prowl, I know my culinary choices will be endless.

About 30 miles north of town, I take Route 12 west over to Route 155 south and soon find myself officially on the tour. I am pleasantly surprised to discover I'm riding on one of Tallahassee's famed Canopy Roads, originally old Indian trails that later became market roads. Plantation owners lined the roads with live oaks that have since grown over the road, their branches intertwining. Spanish moss has taken a liking to these surroundings and hangs copiously from the limbs. The sunshine filtering through the porous archway seemingly springs to life, partnered to sway in the warm Florida breeze with the grayish-green filaments. I vastly enjoy exploring these canopy roads. But my schedule says otherwise. It's good to know that the state law protects Tallahassee's Canopy Roads. They'll be around for years to come.

Forging ever closer to town, Route 155 becomes North Meridian Road. Eventually houses, condos, and lots of cars replace the live oaks. The warm day heating up the bumper-to-bumper traffic has me rethinking lunch, and the decision to escape the throngs of harried drivers, all seemingly late for class, comes easily. I find Route 20 and head west.

A quick, tasty bite of spicy-sweet brisket at a local barbeque hangout just outside of town has me reenergized and ready to tackle the afternoon. Despite the bellyful of tender beef, I know that somewhere south of here a number of poor, unsuspecting oysters are being rudely pried from their bed. Dinner tonight will be compliments of a hard-working waterman's tongs.

I pick up Route 375 south and hope to get a good feel for Florida's wild lands with a ride through the Apalachicola National Forest. What I get doesn't feel all that great. The road is flat, straight, and it offers little in the way of scenery save millions of pine trees. For miles and miles the road is nothing but an elongated triangle stretched out directly in front of the bike, its point eternally obscured by distant, liquescent heat waves.

After what seems an eternity, a short stint on Route 319 ends at Route 98. I'm looking at the Gulf of Mexico. Heading west toward Carabelle, I'm amazed by how calm the water is. No waves at all, not even a ripple. The fact that this area of the coast is lightly populated adds to the serenity; and the slant of the afternoon sun has the few boats on the water looking like they're perched atop a huge mirror.

The short ride along the coast grants a brief respite from the drab, inland scenery, and I dread my northward turn on Route 67. I'm right. The featureless road seems scarcely more than an excuse to have laid asphalt through pine trees. Thankfully, the loop only takes an hour and the Gulf is again coming into sight. By now, the sunset is in full glory and the rays are putting on a free light show.

Sailing across the bridge into Apalachicola, I'm beginning to feel the toll that two days of hard riding have

taken. I'll be staying the night at the Gibson Inn, the first building I see as I pull into town. The lobby is absolutely beautiful. Done in warm, rich woods, it oozes both charm and history. I think I'm going to like this place. As I'm

○ *Oysters. Bring me more oysters.*

to travel far before I'm situated at the bar of the Apalachicola Seafood Grill and waiting for oysters with a side of oysters. A couple dozen delectable bivalves and a beer or two later, I find myself wandering back to the inn, soaking

○ *A tranquil scene along one of Tallahassee's canopy roads.*

checking in, I hear that I've just missed the innkeepers, who've gone out for a motorcycle ride. At least I know I'm in good hands. It's not long before I head out on foot to find my oysters. I don't have

in the warm gulf breeze and the comfortable ambiance of this working-class waterfront community. There's a feeling in the air that things around here haven't changed much over the years.

When I get back to the inn, I find the innkeepers have returned with several of their riding buddies. Conversation ranges from area history and restaurant recommendations to extended discussions about riding and custom Harley-

↺ *Heading home with the afternoon catch.*

↻ *Checking the map in the shade of a sprawling oak.*

Davidsons. Finally, exhausted, I retire upstairs to my cushy four-poster bed and drift off wondering if the sea captain's ghost will visit tonight. Request room 309 and they'll tell you all about it.

Another Day, Another Oyster

A dense fog thwarts an early start. Oh well, more time to enjoy this cozy bed. Finally on my way, I backtrack a bit to St. George Island State Park where I'm treated to a truly beautiful and unique ocean-side nature sanctuary. The water and protected sand dunes are home to a plethora of unique critters, and the park service has done a great job of marrying accessibility with nature. On my way out I see the watermen at work gathering oysters. It looks like hard work, and I vow to continue doing my part to support the local economy.

I remember someone telling me about the Indian Pass Raw Bar. I'm following signs to the Indian Pass community, so I must be on the right path. I finally see a weather-beaten sign for the Raw Bar and as so many others have surely done, I ride right by. There was a building there but it looked like an old closed general store. A quick U-turn reveals that the worn-down building is indeed the Indian Pass Raw Bar. Entering the joint, I chuckle about the notion of suggesting they place a billboard down the road that reads: "Aw, shucks! Y'all just passed the Indian Pass Raw Bar." But I soon shelved the idea of disclosing any such ad copy after gauging the ticked-off mood of the rather large proprietor conversing with two equally huge fellows regarding the foibles of the local high school's football program. I mean, if he's happy with his advertising, I am too.

It's all about the food anyway. So trust me on this one: The contents of this book bear no resemblance to its cover. I had an early lunch of a dozen baked oysters that were simply some of the best I've ever had. They're doing something right and it shouldn't be missed.

I'm not too far from St. Josephs Peninsula State Park. It's widely recognized as one of the best beaches in the United States and a visit makes it easy to understand why. The snow-white sand is lapped by crystal clear water that takes on almost unreal shades of blue, green, and turquoise away from the shore. Development has been curtailed, allowing the beach to retain its natural beauty; and though the park is a bit off the beaten path, it's worth the extra ride.

◗ Panhandle history and pride inside.

◗ The Indian Pass Raw bar is a local institution.

Another boring inland loop and severe traffic in Panama City has me a bit frazzled as the day draws to a close. Here is where seaside becomes "the beach." Four lanes, high rises, water parks, go-kart tracks, theme restaurants, and those shops that sell "custom" air-brushed tee shirts of sunset-silhouetted palm trees framing an announcement that 'somebody loves somebody' rule the scene. I like the coast, but I'm not much for the beach. I head inland to find a room for the evening.

Who Turned Off the Heat?

Getting an early start on day three, I'm thankful I remembered to pack my First Heat electric vest. A cold, windy ride awaits along a pretty stretch of beach near Destin and Fort Walton Beach that remains somewhat desolate due to its function as a military installation. The windblown white sands have an almost Arctic appearance. As the military base abruptly ends, the condos begin. Ride on sez me.

I again head north on Route 87 at Navarre. The dreaded inland ride is now mired with road construction. Bigger roads shuttle more people. But once 87 clears Interstate 10 the ride becomes surprisingly nice. Farms dot the landscape, providing welcome relief from the interminable pine forests. East on Route 4, where a leisurely ride back down toward the water begins, and I was hoping for one last stab at some seafood along Choctawhatchee Bay, but I'm rewarded only with scenery. I stop at a tiny place along the way and choose another source of protein. What a great cheeseburger they make here. The tomatoes are thick and the fries hot and fresh. Ah, much better – let's go do some riding.

The route north through De Funiak Springs up to Route 2 is a sure sign that there's still plenty of country left in Florida. The traffic is light and the folks are friendly. These are the kind of roads that make any tour enjoyable. I still have a respectable amount of daylight left as I head south on Route 271. Lake Seminole glimmers through the trees on my left. A number of people are fishing this afternoon and almost all give a wave.

The final leg of the tour is an east-ward trek on Route 90. Small towns and farms chase monotony from the straight roads. Cows stare and kids shout and wave as I motor by. The town of Quincy surprises me with some of the prettiest homes I've seen in a long time. They conjure the Old South with their stout columns, tall windows, and solid white exteriors. The wrought iron fences, neat yards, and the omnipresent Spanish moss-hung oaks give Quincy the appearance of a town unconcerned with the passage of time.

Not too far from Quincy, I come to the stop sign that marks my starting point. The Florida Panhandle is, without a doubt, a land of extremes. In a matter of a few days, I've seen a relaxed Apalachicola and a wide-open Tallahassee, crystal Gulf waters and the cola-colored Blackwater River, leisurely country lanes and mind-numbing straights through the pine forests, the southern charm of Quincy and the oceanfront high rises in Destin. There's definitely something for every taste. When you go, bring several different hats, because you never know where the end of the day may have you.

Florida Panhandle
FACTS AND INFORMATION

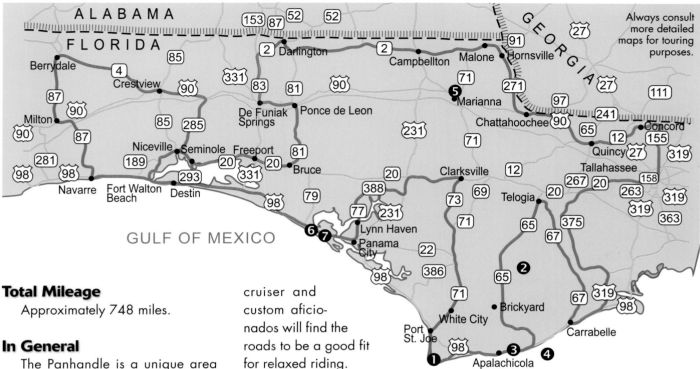

Always consult more detailed maps for touring purposes.

Total Mileage

Approximately 748 miles.

In General

The Panhandle is a unique area given the general impression of the Sunshine State. Most folks think of Disney World, South Beach, and Key West when Florida enters the discussion. Although the Destin, Panama Beach, and Fort Walton Beach areas do offer the usual tourist fare, these places are the exception. Expect a laid-back attitude and Old South country charm.

Travel Season

Winter is generally mild, but cold snaps happen. Summer is hot – it is Florida after all. Be sure to have your swim gear handy. The crystal clear waters and sparsely populated beaches may inspire an impromptu dip. To avoid the humidity and mid-afternoon rainstorms associated with summer, try planning your trip in March or April.

Roads & Biking

Generally, the roads in the Panhandle are long and straight, with few curves. Sport riders will not be impressed, but cruiser and custom aficionados will find the roads to be a good fit for relaxed riding.

The western and northern inland roads are just fine to ride and the farms, small towns, and interesting people offer pleasant distractions from the straight-bored asphalt. On the whole, the roads are in excellent shape, but when near the coast, watch out for sand, especially if the wind is blowing.

Food & Lodging

Aside from oysters and shrimp, and mullet (a local specialty), all sorts of fresh fish are readily available. Barbecue pits and small cafes operate all over. Finding a room can be dicey, depending on the season. And bear in mind, the Panhandle seasons run counter to south Florida's. Here, the off-season is the winter, and the summers are busy. Call ahead in warm weather.

Maps

o AAA - Florida State Road Map
o *Rand McNally 2007 Road Atlas Florida*
   Rand McNally & Company
   ISBN 0528859277, $24.95

More Information

o Florida Online Park Guide
   www.floridastateparks.org
o Apalachicola Chamber of Commerce
   www.apalachicola.org
o Florida Panhandle Travel and
   Tourist Information
   www.visitfloridaonline.com/visit_
   florida_panhandle.htm

Attractions

❶ St. Joseph Peninsula State Park
   (850) 227-1327
❷ Apalachicola National Forest
   (850) 643-2282
❸ Crooked River Lighthouse
   (850) 697-8148
❹ St. George Island State Park
   (850)927-2111
❺ Florida Caverns State Park
   (850) 482-9598
❻ Gulf World Marine Park
   (850) 234-5271
❼ SeaBreeze Winery, (850) 230-330

Shamrock Tour® – Kentucky

Riding The Green Tunnels in Daniel Boone Country

Two-lane asphalt snakes its way through steep mountain gorges sculpted over millions of years by rushing streams. Lush vegetation presses in from all sides, often overarching the road and blotting out the sun. My feet and hands move with practiced precision, downshifting, tapping the brakes, leaning deeply into the curves, rolling on the throttle and up-shifting through the gears as the motorcycle gathers speed. My complete attention is focused on the constantly curving yellow line threading its way through a tunnel of green.

Text: James T. Parks
Photography: Christian Neuhauser

After enduring several days of rain at the Honda Hoot in Knoxville, Tennessee, my wife Karen and I are elated by the prospect of sunshine favoring our four-day Shamrock tour in eastern Kentucky. We rendezvous with Christian and Christa at the Cumberland Inn in Williamsburg, Kentucky, a small college town of 5,000. Gleefully, over a late dinner there, Christian lays out his preview of the maniacal combination of curvy routes he's stitched together for our eastern Kentucky adventure.

Big South Fork Loop: 180 miles

Before departing the following morning, I double-check the tread depth on my 2004 Honda ST1300 and find that it should be ready for anything that Christian, the "Route Meister," is likely to throw at us. Pulling out of the parking lot, his Aprilia Falco leads us south on US 25W. Christa follows next on the Kawasaki Concours, and my wife and I bring up the rear, riding two-up on the Honda.

In the cool morning air, I recall that the cloud-shrouded mountains in this southeast corner of Kentucky, with their steep slopes and dense forests, kept early colonists from settling here for nearly 150 years. Although Indians had used a natural passage through the mountain barrier for centuries, the Cumberland Gap's location was not documented until 1750. Daniel Boone led a work party of 30 axmen in 1775 to mark what became known as The Wilderness Road, which lead settlers to the fabled Bluegrass Region in central Kentucky.

Crossing the border into Tennessee, our route becomes State Road (SR) 297, which takes us west to the Big South Fork National River and Recreation Area. It's situated in a rugged gorge area of the Cumberland Plateau that straddles southern Kentucky and northeastern Tennessee. Our descent into the gorge is steep, with

○ *A kind stranger provides shelter from a pounding rainstorm.*

tight, second-gear curves. Shear red rock walls line both sides of the road, and I'm finding it challenging to stay on pace with the effortlessly smooth movements of the two motorcycles in front of us. Over the next four days, though, literally thousands of curves will help refine my riding skills.

The most obvious geological features observed in this area are the numerous rock overhangs which provided shelter to early settlers and moonshiners in later times. The stable dry soils underneath the overhangs have yielded archeologists well-preserved specimen's of bone, leather and other organic materials.

We pass briefly into and out of the Central Time Zone as we head north on Tennessee SR 154, which becomes SR 167 in Kentucky. By the time we reach Monticello, Kentucky, everyone is feeling strong hunger pains. Following the Neuhauser doctrine of avoiding fast-food chain restaurants wherever and whenever possible, we discover a home-cooked buffet at a restaurant on SR 90.

Exiting the building, we're greeted by temperatures in the eighties and higher humidity. Our return trip to Monticello follows sweeping curves in the Daniel Boone National Forest through what I dub the green tunnels. Steep valleys covered with lush plant life largely restrict our vision of the two-lane asphalt and its yellow centerline, continuously disappearing around blind curves.

The Figure Eight Loop: 165 miles

The second day's planned ride makes a figure eight, with its first loop east of Williamsburg and the second one west of town. This will allow us to have lunch midway in Williamsburg. Attempting to rouse Karen for breakfast, she sleepily informs me that she will join us on the afternoon loop, but to please enjoy myself on the morning loop. I was more than a little jealous of her extra snooze time in the queen-sized bed.

Christa and I trade bikes for the first few hours of the trip. I find the Kawasaki Concours to be a lot of fun. Departing Williamsburg on SR 92 east, it's not long before we get into some serious canyon carving.

A right on SR 904 soon presents us with our first major navigational challenge. Rounding a curve, we find our route abruptly turns into a gravel road of undetermined length. We're consulting our map for an alternate route when a helpful fellow in a pickup truck stops. He's certain the gravel lasts only a little while, not more than a mile at most. Riding my 700-pound ST 1300 on the gravel is a little like being on the back of a rhinoceros on ice skates – powerful and fleet on solid ground, it becomes ungainly out of its element. Maintaining a speed of between 10 and 15 mph, the one-mile off-road experience turns out to be a slow two-mile traverse on the gravel.

One of the most exciting roads of the morning is SR 225. This narrow switchback twist-a-thon, up and over a mountain ridge, has us tossing our bikes left and right in rapid succession on a green route completely overarched with vegetation.

We stop in the sleepy little town of Barbourville for a break and refreshment. Striding into the Dairy Queen in leathers and textile riding gear, we receive those

↻ *Exiting one of the many green tunnels on the tour.*

PREVENT FOREST FIRES

◯ *Climbing to the sky on the Coal Country Loop.*

"you're not from these parts" stares from the local patrons, but they soon go back to contemplating their milkshakes.

Refreshed, we follow a very twisty SR 6 and then SR 459, taking us in a big circle back to Barbourville. With darkening skies, we hurriedly follow SR 11 and SR 779, managing to dodge most of the rain on our way back to Williamsburg for lunch.

With the sun again shining brightly, and Karen now on the back of the ST, we pursue the western half of the figure eight route on SR 92 and SR 1044. We trace the path of small streams through heavily forested valleys and negotiate switchbacks up and over mountain ridges in the Daniel Boone National Forest.

Motoring back east on SR 478, we enjoy one sweeping curve after another that can be taken at speed just by leaning the bike over. The combination of green tunnels and continuous curves, produce a pleasant Zen-like state, and I mentally dub this particular stretch "sweeper heaven." We cap off

the day's events with a dip in the pool and a nice long soak of sore muscles in the hot tub.

Coal Country Loop: 135 miles

Our third loop turns out to be the shortest but the most technically challenging. Heading south out of Williamsburg on US 25W, we arrive in Jellico, Tennessee, where we pick up SR 90 west, which turns into SR 74 in Kentucky.

The stretch of SR 74 between Fonde, Kentucky, and Middlesboro, Kentucky, requires our total concentration. Virtually all of the tight switchback curves are negotiated in second gear as we tread lightly on pavement with a thin covering of coal dust. We stay highly alert to avoid oncoming coal trucks, taking up their lane and part of ours, and the large potholes on the right edge of the road, which threaten to catapult the unwary over a low guardrail and down the mountainside.

We overtake a coal truck lumbering up a steep grade at about 10 or 15 mph. After riding in a cloud of coal dust in first

gear for several minutes, we look for an opportunity to pass. The courteous truck driver finally signals with his left turn indicator that the coast is clear, but we wait until we can actually see empty pavement before launching around him. The downward slope is only slightly less demanding, as we keep an eye on the rearview for the possibility of trucks rapidly coming up behind with overheated brakes.

Rolling into Middlesboro, Christian directs us to a rustic café for our well-earned lunch break. We briefly consider following US 25E through the tunnel under Cumberland Mountain to the Cumberland Gap Visitor's Center, but decide to save that destination for a future Tennessee tour.

The afternoon ride has us heading east along the northern base of Cumberland Mountain on SR 217 and then back west along the southern base of Pine Mountain in Kentucky Ridge State Forest on the ever-twisty SR 190.

Pine Mountain is a 25-mile-long ridge stretching northwest near Jellico, Tennessee to Elkhorn City, Kentucky. It's the direct result of a geological fault, called the Pine Mountain Thrust Fault, which caused a large block of the earth's crust to be pushed up and over the area that is now southeastern Kentucky.

We take a somewhat rough SR 1595 through a gap in Pine Mountain and then catch SR 92 east. We pause for a photo op along a particularly scenic section of SR 92, and as Christa and I turn around in a driveway for another pass before the camera, we're suddenly surrounded by living remnants of the Aztec civilization – a barking pack of crazed chihuahuas. Fortunately, there's no way they can jump high enough to even reach our foot pegs. So, we escape with our lives and get the picture!

Lake Country Loop: 184 miles

The final loop of our Shamrock tour takes us north to the Laurel River Lake area and beyond. Following SR 204, the ride begins with high fog and a few light sprinkles. We pause at the dam on SR 1193 to gaze upon the lake as shafts of sunlight finally break through the cloud cover. The roads on this route are a virtual racetrack. Sweeping curves, which can be taken in fourth gear, help us maintain a consistent, rapid pace.

Throttling back and downshifting through the gears, we cruise into Somerset, Kentucky, and find that we're in for a pleasant surprise. Unlike many of the other small towns on our routes, which have seen better days, the historic buildings in downtown Somerset are nicely preserved and there is vibrancy in the step of town residents. Once we negotiate the turns around the town square, our eyes widen when we spot a very cool-looking coffee house.

Stepping inside for coffee and scones, we are greeted by an almost European ambiance. Another patron, catching a few phrases of German between Christian and Christa, tells us that he is from Holland and has been living in this area for the past 20 years. He informs us that around 150,000 boating enthusiasts from Ohio descend on Laurel Lake on summer weekends, which explains the more prosperous appearance of Somerset.

Reluctantly, we bid farewell to Somerset and continue our journey north on SR 39. A series of three- and four-digit winding back roads take us through more open and scenic countryside, eventually depositing us in London, Kentucky, for lunch. Again, following the Neuhauser back-road dining doctrine, we find the quaint Weaver's Restaurant on Main Street. They have extensive menu selections, as long as you want either a hamburger or a hot dog, but the price of $3.50 for food and drink is unbeatable.

A young man at a nearby table, deducing from our dress and full-face helmets that we're long-distance motorcyclists, asks the question we get at almost every stop, "Where are you coming from?" "We started in Williamsburg," I reply. And then the inevitable, "Where are you going?" "Well, we're on our way back to Williamsburg, which is where we're staying," I inform him. A look of confusion follows as he asks, "So, you're just going in circles?" "Yes," I reply, "that pretty much sums it up."

Winding our way back to Williamsburg, I realize that our eastern Kentucky four-day, back-road curve-a-thon is almost over. Even after negotiating thousands of curves over the last four days, I'm still trying to perfect my entrance and exit on each of those that remain. We are racing against, and into, darkening clouds that threaten heavy rain. We don't quite make it to Williamsburg before the sky opens up on us. A kind man at a fruit stand lets us take refuge under an awning while the rain beats down mercilessly. Although it's raining on the last few miles of our tour, we're all happy and content from four wonderful days of riding in the sunshine.

Rounding another curve in the cooling shade of great, green trees.

FACTS AND INFORMATION

Total Mileage

Approximately 616 miles.

In General

Welcome to Daniel Boone country! Eastern Kentucky is a mountainous and heavily forested area bisected by steep-walled gorges and sheer rock cliffs. Secondary roads follow the serpentine paths of the many streams that have sculpted the region's geography for eons. The seemingly endless progression of curves is a sport motorcyclist's nirvana.

Travel Season

Due to high temperatures and humidity during summer months, spring and fall are the best times to travel this area by motorcycle. The benefit of riding in autumn, of course, is witnessing the magnificent tunnels of green turn to rich shades of orange and yellow.

Roads & Biking

The roads on this tour are well off the beaten path, lightly traveled, and exceptionally curvy. Road surfaces are generally good, but there are some rough spots that pop up unexpectedly – and remember, on gravel, to use only the rear brake. This tour takes place mostly on three- and four-digit secondary roads, so ordinary road maps are virtually useless for trying to follow the many road changes.

Maps

○ *The Roads of Kentucky*, Mapsco ISBN 1569664242, $19.95

More Information

○ The Kentucky Department of Travel www.kentuckytourism.com
○ Williamsburg, Kentucky Tourism www.williamsburgky.com

Attractions

❶ Cumberland Gap National Historical Park (606) 248-2817
❷ Chained Rock, Pine Mountain State Resort Park (606) 337-3066
❸ Cedar Creek Vineyards (606) 274-1964
❹ Bear Wallow Farm (606) 871-7745
❺ Kentucky Music Hall of Fame (606) 256-1000
❻ Historic BitterSweet Cabin Village (606) 256-9814

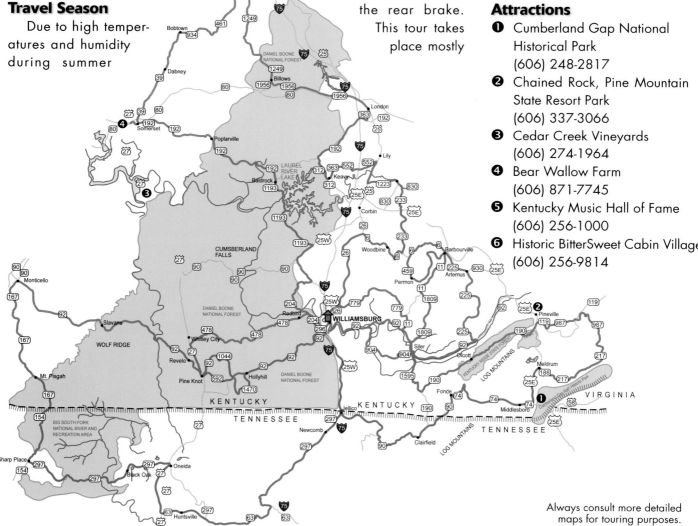

Always consult more detailed maps for touring purposes.

WHEN THE PAVEMENT ENDS

If you do enough motorcycle touring, sooner or later you'll end up where the tarmac turns to dirt. You'll need to modify your riding technique to stay upright, especially when surface conditions change. In fact, that's about the only predictable characteristic of off-road riding: it's unpredictable.

Slipping and Sliding

The first thing you notice on a loose surface is reduced traction. If you accelerate and steer and brake the way you would on tarmac, the bike will eventually slide out from under you; giving the bike the correct inputs will keep you upright. You'll also notice that the steering seems heavier, a result of an increased contact patch as the front tire sinks into the surface. Keep the bike upright, point the front wheel where you want to go, and steer with the throttle.

Say what? It seems bizarre, but on loose surfaces, it matters much less what the rear wheel is doing than the front. The rear wheel may drift out slightly as you accelerate through a turn, but that just helps point you in the right direction.

Stand up!

Perhaps the single most useful technique you can learn for off-road riding is standing on the pegs. This has the effect of lowering the overall center of gravity of bike and rider. When you're standing, your weight goes through the pegs, applying your mass to the bottom of the frame, pushing the center of gravity down. This not only makes the bike more stable on the loose surface, but also allows you to apply steering inputs by shifting your weight on the pegs.

Speed and Gearing

Finding the right speed is important for off-road riding. At first, you'll want to crawl along, but as you push yourself to go faster, you'll find the bike responds better and feels way less squirrelly. Of course, going too fast is also a problem, because braking and changing direction needs much more anticipation than on pavement. Make sure you can actually see far enough ahead to stop.

Being in the right gear is also important. Choosing a gear that's too low makes throttle control more difficult, especially on rough surfaces. I usually ride a gear higher than I would on tarmac for the same speed. Remember, though, that you'll still need to be in the power band so you have acceleration when you need it. Going down-hill, drop a gear or two and use the engine to slow you down. It's much easier than trying to accurately control just the rear brake.

Sand

Few things are more disconcerting than riding a motorcycle in deep sand for the first time. The front wheel will plow left and right, seemingly impervious to your attempts to steer, threatening to throw you off. When you hit a patch of sand, shift your weight back on the seat and open the throttle to accelerate through it. This reduces weight on the front wheel, which will tend to "float" through the sand rather than getting bogged down in it.

Water

Before you ford a stream, park your bike and take a good look at the water. If it's rippling, there's a good chance it's fairly shallow. If it's not, and you can't see the bottom, walk through first to see how deep it is. Below carburetor height and you're probably okay. But don't stall the engine or you may suck water into the exhaust. Go slowly in first gear, slipping the clutch and keeping the revs high.

OK – now you're ready to practice!

Appalachian Trails

6053 FT.
HIGHEST ELEVATION
BLUE RIDGE PARKWAY
MOTOR ROAD

UNITED STATES DEPARTMENT OF THE INTERIOR
NATIONAL PARK SERVICE

Along the Skyline Drive
and Blue Ridge Parkway

Text and Photography: Christian Neuhauser

Most riders and drivers prefer to wait for autumn's cavalcade of color for scenic tours along the Skyline Drive and Blue Ridge Parkway. In the summer, these outrageous roads are packed full when loads of city slickers escape the lowland humidity for picnics and maybe some napping in the shade of high country trees. Me? I usually like to travel there during the quieter days of spring, especially in the month of April.

Ice and Snow

This trip out, I've chosen a very unusual motorcycle brand. Our companions are a Royal Enfield Bullet and the brand-new Sixty-5. Steve Benson, my riding buddy, rolled the bikes off the showroom floor and brought them down in his trailer from his Shreve, Ohio dealership. We met during the Cleveland Motorcycle Show and then and there started planning this particular udventure.

We unload the bikes in a cold drizzle in Front Royal, Virginia. The thermometer reads 42 degrees. But when you have the right riding gear everything is roger. Stoically, Steve pulls his FirstGear rain gear over his jeans and his checkered lumberjack jacket. I've been ready to roll, and watch as Steve arranges his ZZ-Top beard. Finally, we start 'em up and the Royal Enfield singles roll out of the city toward the ramp to the Skyline Drive.

At the northern entrance station I pay ten bucks for both bikes. Today's route is 105 miles to Rockfish Gap at the end of the Skyline Drive. Immediately the road snakes and winds upward steeply. The grayish ribbon soon becomes one with the fog and disappears. We can barely see the centerline. The ranger at the entrance notified us that restaurants along the Skyline Drive are closed; so, we're on our own. Ten miles in, we reach Compton Gap (2,145ft.) and snowflakes drop from the dense fog. Suddenly I see a shadowy figure and pull on the brake lever, approaching slowly. A deer herd, a group at least 15 strong, blocks the road. We pass cautiously, expecting more of the same in these weather conditions. After an hour, 45 miles, we pull in at Upper Hawksbill Parking at 3,630 feet. I had to stop; I'm frozen, chilled to the marrow. So, I try to warm up a bit by sprinting around the bikes a few times. Steve, amused by my an-

tics, finally takes pity and opens his left saddlebag to pull out a thermos of hot tea. There follows a nice warm toast to the man who has thought of everything.

Eventually cruising downward, the atmosphere noticeably warmer with each 500-foot drop in elevation, we cheer up and the drizzle stops. Blue spots chink the blanketing bank of clouds. By five we arrive in Waynesboro, Virginia, and find a nice clean spot for rest at the Super 8 Motel. Pradip Pandit, the manager, is from India and his eyes sparkle when spotting the Royal Enfields.

↻ Another wonderful Parkway vista in western NC.

The Longest Day

The blue skies and bright sunshine are most welcome, but not so the stiff cold breeze that shoulders its way inside when we open the door in the morning. The sign across the road says it's 33 degrees.

Brutal riding. And I'm trussed up like the Michelin Man: three T-shirts, a sweater and my Belstaff wax jacket. It all helps a bit. The first miles are tough, but soon the body gets used to the punishment, and the soul considers other excitement. Six miles down the road, we turn onto the Blue Ridge Parkway.

Created as one of the New Deal's projects during the Great Depression, the Blue Ridge Parkway winds 469 miles through Virginia and North Carolina. In 1939, just over 100,000 people visited the Parkway; today, during peak season in October, 2.5 to 3 million people will travel here. To avoid this "battle on the road," I prefer April when the pavement is almost empty, when no caravans of flatlanders in huge cars are doing 15 miles an hour to interrupt a smooth and fluid ride.

Steve and I are focused on signs of wildlife crossing. Every now and then more deer, a turkey, and once a rabbit intersect our lines. Occasionally a car or other bikers pass by. The trees are still naked, revealing views you normally don't see. Ponds and rushing creeks are reassuring indications of the next few curves.

Mileposts line the length of the Parkway and, after crossing Otter Creek (649ft.), the lowest point along the route at MP 60.9 and the James River at MP 63.6, we stop for lunch at the Peaks of Otter Lodge. Neither of us is very, hungry but this upscale spot is certainly worth a stop for a stretch and look-see. The mountain resort, open year-round, offers comfortable lodging and a great view overlooking Abbott Lake and Sharp Top Mountain.

○ *Afternoon shadows, a lovely roadside meadow.*

Soon we're back in the swing of things, having a pleasant ride. Our Enfields roll through the corners like it was nothing. The handling is so easy and even though producing only 22 horsepower, the bikes are strong enough to sweep over the mountains.

Near MP 120, we pass Roanoke, VA, the former home of the Parkway headquarters. This mountain city, well known for its lively downtown, has a century-old open-air farmers' market and a national-model cultural center worth stopping to see.

From there to Tuggles Gap for our lunch, it's another exciting ride. Midway through those 41 miles, the Bullet frightens me with a loud *Klong* noise. I check the mirror. The Bullet's muffler

sprawls on the road. Steve had already stopped. He picks up the piece and immediately drops it in the grass – yeah, it's hot. Inspecting the brackets, we see I've lost two screws. His imperturbable good humor intact, Steve scrambles about to jerry-rig repairs by cannibalizing enough screws from my seat. It works.

Stomachs constricted to the point of pain, we arrive at Tuggles Gap, a local biker hangout on Highway 8 and only half a mile away from the Parkway. Having lived nearby in Winston-Salem for some time, I know this spot well. It's one of my favorite "eateries" – great homemade food, friendly service and very reasonable prices.

Steve arches an eyebrow when he hears my rapid-fire order. "Wow, you

must really know this menu," he says. "What can you recommend?"

"Everything is delicious," I answer, thinking about the special American burger and "yummy" coconut cream cake that's coming. "Some weekends Christa, the boys and I ride here just for the cake. We call it the Coconut Rally." Fooling around and gorging ourselves, it's almost three o'clock when we hit the road for Boone.

We stop for a short break at Mr. Ed Mabry's mill. He must be a relation of Steve's. People around here still talk about how Mabry could fix most anything at his combination sawmill, gristmill, and blacksmith shop. He ran the establishment from 1910 to 1935. Today, Mabry Mill – with demonstrations of the old-time skills of

○ *"High" guys met on 215, a twisty Parkway side road.*

basket weaving, seat caning, spinning and weaving presented – is an attraction every Parkway explorer should experience.

Just before MP 217, we cross the border between Virginia and North Carolina. The road winds through rolling farm country, fields and forests. Beyond the visitor center at Cumberland Knob, we pull over at the Fox Hunters Paradise Overlook. This magnificent view extends panoramically over steep, tree-covered bluffs toward the gentler slopes of North Carolina's Piedmont (foothills).

South of Cumberland Knob, the Blue Ridge Parkway curves gently through lovely meadows and passes into blustery Air Bellows Gap, where the Sixty-5 drops *its* muffler. But Steve expertly figures out how to manage without it. And sunset finds us in more comfortable circumstances, 100 miles away, at the Holiday Inn Express in Boone, NC. The day's total: 340 miles.

Conclusive Cruise

After a great breakfast from the buffet, we saddle up and ride towards Cherokee. The weather is good, warm enough, and the riding smooth. On the ancient slopes of Grandfather Mountain, a few miles farther along, the first signs of the spruce-fir forest in North Carolina high country appear. Deep, dark green swatches. The Linn Cove Viaduct, a stupefying feat of engineering, bends gracefully around the eastern slope of the peak. But the asphalt is brittle, requiring a lot of attention. In a word, dropping over any one of the soaring seven pillars supporting the roadbed is suicide. Constructed this way to avoid environmental damage to Hugh Morton's Grandfather Mountain, the quarter-mile-long viaduct is made of 153 individually designed segments, and it was dedicated in 1987, marking the official completion of the Blue Ridge Parkway, 52 years after the work began.

Near Little Switzerland, blithely circling the bikes through great sweepers, we suddenly venture upon an insurmountable obstacle: Road Closed. All the way to Asheville. This interruption of our run is most unappreciated, but nothing is stopping us from substituting a race to Mount Mitchell State Park. Soon our disappointment is all but forgotten after an unbridled ride down Hwy 80. It's full of switchbacks and plenty of challenging corners, and once we reach Black Mountain we're glad we had to detour.

Steve's eyes are practically bulging from the sockets when we stop in the parking lot of a restaurant, and enthusiasm bubbles so quickly from his lips I have to laugh. He's almost babbling, telling me repeatedly how that has to be the best road he's ridden in his life.

Time passes quite enjoyably over a delicious meal and a sidecar of biker stories before we take 70 to rejoin the Parkway and scoot past Asheville, the only other major city on this mountain route. Taking over from Roanoke, Asheville is now home to the new Parkway headquarters. It's also the site of the majestic Biltmore Estate, the venerable Grove Park Inn, and a thriving downtown.

Sweepers and tight corners spoil us on the way to the highest point of our ride. At Richland Balsam, the Parkway climbs to an elevation of 6,047 feet where the forest that whizzes by seems a very convincing replication of Canada's wilderness. Photos snapped and curves pulling us down to Waterrock Knob, a wild chase hurtles us toward MP 443.1 and the US 19 intersection. Rhythmically winding over the road

◔ Stopping to admire the hazy rolling hills of Piedmont North Carolina.

159

○ *Well-maintained asphalt, curves and beautiful surroundings– what more could one ask for?*

○ *Mabry Mill is an old gristmill still in operation an MP 176.1*

through the Pisgah National Forest, the bikes are running great today, almost as if trying to make up for yesterday's bad behavior.

Six miles beyond Waterrock Knob, we enter the Cherokee Indian Reservation. This illustrious tribe has lived in these highlands for untold generations, and dozens of place names reflect that heritage, including nearby Lake Junaluska and the Nantahala Forest.

Twenty-six miles left to the end of this day's journey, I always enter this area respectfully, reflecting on the tragedies that unfolded here two centuries ago. For all their trust and help, an entire nation was grievously betrayed, forced from their land and marched 1,200 miles on "The Trail of Tears" to Oklahoma. Ironically, Cherokee Chief Junaluska had once saved the life of the President who engineered this genocidal trek (some 4,000 men, women and children died along the way from disease and exposure). Chief Junaluska, fighting alongside the Americans, is credited with pulling Andrew Jackson's fat from the fire at the Battle of Horseshoe Bend in 1812. Today, you can learn more about those times and Cherokee history in the outdoor drama "Unto These Hills," in the Oconaluftee Indian Village and the Museum of the Cherokee Indian.

Running late, we arrive past closing – although the casino's still drawing a crowd – and take Hwy 19 back to Waynesville, the point of tomorrow's departure for home. Again, it's been one for the books. Very little traffic, great vistas, and beautiful weather during these last two April days have all conspired to create another outrageous ride through the "Land of the Blue Mist."

FACTS AND INFORMATION

Total Mileage

Approximately 573 miles.

In General

The Shenandoah Skyline Drive and the Blue Ridge Parkway are two of the most well-traveled roads in the eastern United States. These scenic routes are crowded in summer when people are looking for some cool relaxation at higher elevation; and in autumn, when the area is inundated with leaf-peepers, with unending caravans of steel snaking over the mountains. It's quietest in winter, but hazardous conditions preclude most bike trips by then.

Indian and pathfinder trails before becoming roads, they lead through much of the historical landscape of Virginia and North Carolina. Museums, battlefields and other significant landmarks await your discovery around almost every corner in these states.

Travel Season

Spring is a wonderful time for explorations here. Temperatures are just starting to get warm and without the crowds the fall and summer attract, there's more room to freely enjoy the technical aspects of the ride.

Roads & Biking

The Skyline Drive and The Blue Ridge Parkway are without doubt the most scenic roadways in the East. They are well maintained, but don't expect to zip along and miss the views – the speed limit on the Skyline Drive is 35mph; on the Parkway it's 45mph. Deer and quickly changing weather situations are some of the challenges facing riders on this scenic north-south connection.

Maps

o *Rand McNally North Carolina Easy Finder: Highways & Interstates* Rand McNally ISBN 0528994824, $7.95

o *American Map Virginia State Road Atlas,* The Map People ADC ISBN 0875307736, $16.95

More Information

o Blue Ridge Parkway (828) 265-4026 www.freetour.virtualblueridge.com
o Little Switzerland www.littleswitzerlandnc.com
o Visit Asheville www.exploreasheville.com
o Boone Convention & Visitors Bureau www.visitboonenc.com
o Virginia Tourism, www.virginia.org

Attractions

❶ Shenandoah National Park (800) 732-0911 (for emergency)
❷ Mabry Mill (276) 952-2947
❸ Biltmore Estate (828) 225-1333

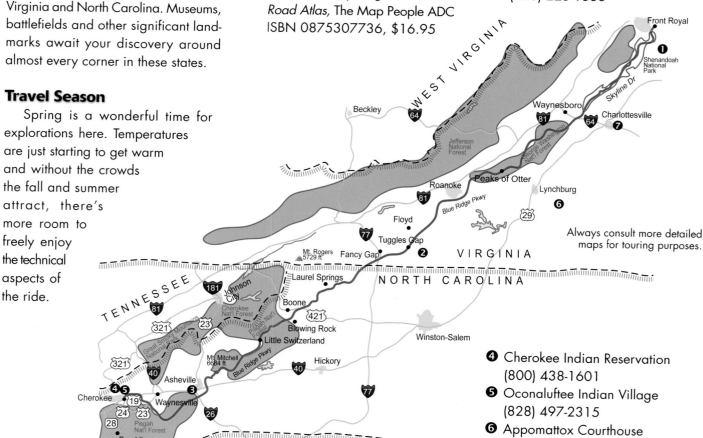

Always consult more detailed maps for touring purposes.

❹ Cherokee Indian Reservation (800) 438-1601
❺ Oconaluftee Indian Village (828) 497-2315
❻ Appomattox Courthouse (434) 352-8987 ext. 26
❼ Thomas Jefferson's Monticello (434) 984-9822

The Southeast

The Northeast

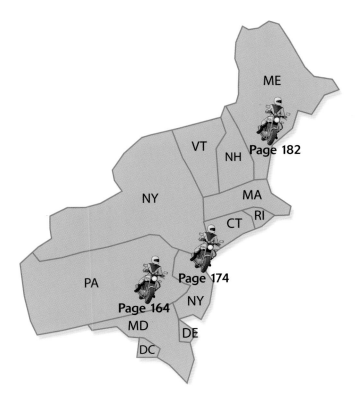

Sunrise is first visible in the U.S. from atop Cadillac Mountain near Bar Harbor, Maine – a stunningly beautiful sight to behold. Although the Northeast is often associated with massive urban developments, it also contains some of the most beautiful scenery in America. The New England States, where colonial America began, have an abundance of charming villages, covered bridges, bucolic farmland, winding country lanes and historical artifacts commemorating the birth of a nation.

The topography of this region was largely influenced by the most recent Ice Age, some 10,000 to 12,000 years ago. Receding glaciers created the rough, rocky shoreline of Maine, the Finger Lakes in New York, the spectacularly scenic Hudson Valley region, Great Lakes Erie and Ontario, the Long Island Sound and many of the other geological marvels that define the northeastern region.

Even more surprising to many visitors to the Northeast are its many remote, wilderness areas, including Pennsylvania's Endless Mountains, New York's Adirondack Park and large tracts of the Pinelands area in central New Jersey. Come and explore this beautifully scenic region with us on some of its enticing two-lane byways.

An Uncommon Wealth Of Fine Riding

Text: Chris Myers
Photography: Chris Myers and Stanley Hansen

Without warning, the clock radio fires a loathsome pop song wreathed in static across the room, piercing my harmonious dream state like a perfectly targeted broadhead arrow burying itself in a dusty hay bale. "Oh Britney, you're frighteningly 'Toxic' at 7:00." But thankfully, the brilliant, blue sky and soothing breeze flowing through the open window quashes my groggy grumbling and spares the offending timepiece a second, unusually heavy-fisted jab at the snooze button.

Despite the rude awakening, I arise surprisingly motivated. The Holiday Inn Express in Harrisburg boasts a nice breakfast spread and I'm ready to do some riding. Having just returned from a week at the annual Americade rally in Lake George, New York, I'm happy to be away from the madding crowds and ready to enjoy some coveted alone time. While rallies are enjoyable, invigorating experiences, I have to admit that a good dose of central Pennsylvania's quiet back roads is just what the doctor ordered.

A Day Of Coal and Cattle

With cinnamon rolls and coffee downed, I fire up the Dyna Super Glide® and romp off into the light, Sunday morning traffic heading toward the Commonwealth's capital. At the broad, rocky Susquehanna River, I bear north on Route 22/322 and the city fades in the rearviews. Peeling off on Route 443, I discover a great road for a morning ride. Smooth pavement and breezy curves lead me through long, wide valleys brimming with fields of corn and grass. The immature maize is barely out of the ground, but with Mother Nature's help, the stalks will soon stretch skyward, making this lane a winding asphalt furrow through an elephant-eye-high sea of green.

North on Routes 125 and 209, the broad expanses give way to forest and steepening hills. At the last minute, I opt for a Pottsville pilgrimage to pay drive-by homage to my favorite sudsy treat, Yuengling Lager. The Yuengling family has been brewing beer here since 1829, and their red brick facility at Fifth and Mahantongo Streets, the oldest brewery in the United States, is listed on the National Register of Historic Places. But of course, on Sunday, I won't need to fight temptation: the brewery is closed.

◖ *Up and over twin bridges.*

Forging east on Route 901, I begin trailing deeper into coal country. Glimpses of tipples, mounds of quarried stone, and massive mining equipment begin to appear through the trees. The small towns are grittier, a little rougher around the edges. There's no artificiality here, and those who have ridden out the good and bad fortunes of the coal industry wear their calluses with pride. NASCAR and Pittsburgh Steelers flags fly high. My kind of place.

Turning south on Route 125 in Shamokin, I stumble across one of those "WOW!" roads that no motorcyclist should miss. Undulating wildly downhill into a steep vale, the serpentine esses suddenly thrust me back into mountain roads full of peg-scraping switchbacks that tax my mettle and metal. Having no desire to push the Super Glide's® envelope, I happily ease over and wave a small group of antsy sport-bike riders by. They all nod appreciatively, screaming past, and quickly disappear around the next curve. I guess I've reached the age where coming home in one piece trumps an adrenaline rush.

Closing in on Klingerstown, I'm loping along on another pastoral, valley road. Wide-eyed calves, not quite knowing what to make of the thumping Harley, clumsily bound away to their mothers' protection. It's best to play it safe and slow down in this area, along Route 25, where Amish buggies routinely share the road. Plus, if you speed by, you'll miss seeing the happy children waving from the rear windows.

Reaching the Susquehanna, I stop for a couple of sloppy but tasty chilidogs at Williams French Fries in Millersburg. I can tell from the confused look of the teenager behind the counter that he's suffering through his first day on the job,

↻ *I had to stop to check out this brake cowliper.*

↻ *Route 125's switchbacks will challenge any machine.*

a situation made all the worse by several of his buddies who've dropped in to razz him. I slide out snickering after one of the young interlopers loudly proclaims that he has been served the worst raspberry ice cream he has ever had – just as the manager walks in. I remember dishing out and receiving such treatment as a youngster and chuckle over the incident all the way back to Harrisburg.

Going Dutch

Another beautiful morning greets me as I rumble south on Route 441 along the Susquehanna. The river valley's rural scenery melds well with the route's rolling hills and effortless curves. Just outside of Royalton, I spot a pair of nuclear power plant cooling towers. This eerie sight becomes especially interesting when I discover I'm riding by *the* Three Mile

Island. Oddly enough, there's actually a roadside marker commemorating the near meltdown that captured worldwide attention back in 1979. And, yes, the plant is still going strong.

Once south of Columbia, the road begins to squirm between the toe of a steep, rocky cliff and the railroad tracks along the riverbank. The further I ride, the smaller Route 441 becomes. Finally it appears to give out altogether in the small town of Mount Nebo. I locate Pennsy Road, which takes me all the way to New Providence across loads of ups, downs, and curves. Bearing south on May Post Office Road, I enter the Pennsylvania Dutch country in earnest.

The Amish, living apart from the modern world, eschew most everyday

◑ *Wide, fertile valleys prevail in central Pennsylvania.*

conveniences including automobiles and electricity in favor of a simpler life. Highly organized and industrious, the sect's convictions are deeply rooted in family, faith, and community. Their small, tidy farms appear one after the other and tractors become a rarity.

Even though it appears to be laundry day in Lancaster County, I'm betting sales at the local appliance store are meager. Clotheslines often stretching fifty feet or more between houses and barns strain under ordered collections of monochromatic garments fluttering in the breeze. In places, these small farms go on as far as the eye can see. Land not being used to graze dairy cows is planted with crops of every sort, and nearly every home has an extensive garden swelling with cabbage, beans, tomatoes, grapes and other staples. All along Routes 897 and 23 real horse power works the land as unassuming, bearded men in black, broad-brimmed hats skillfully maneuver teams pulling farm machinery from another era. Generations of these men and women have

created an idyllic corner of the world here, and it seems to me they've certainly earned the right to tell us *Englishers* to take a hike.

After a delicious visit to the trough at the Shady Maple Smorgasbord in East Earl, I find Route 345 and head

◑ *Pottsville's historic Yuengling brewery.*

north at a fat dog's pace through the French Creek State Park. This protected game land is solid with trees, creating a sudden sensation of tunnel travel beneath the arboreal canopy. Once in Birdsboro, I head west on Route 724 and then turn south again on 568 where the forest is slowly re-

🎧 *A tidy farmhouse in Pennsylvania Dutch country.*

claiming a number of dilapidated, stone-walled barns. Apparently, there's not much farming going on in these hills any more, and the patina of abandonment paints a compelling backdrop beside this narrow, winding road.

As I wind down toward Ephrata, the surroundings again become distinctively agrarian — more rich, wide-open fields. The tarmac tumbles over endless knolls past farm after farm. This area is a produce lover's dream with nearly every driveway sporting signs or stands enticing passersby to share in the bounty.

As I bear north on Route 72, the bucolic landscape gives way to housing construction, new suburbs creeping out from Harrisburg and Hershey. The day's final stretch is Route 22, the old four-lane paralleling Interstate 81. These oft forgotten highways offer fascinating glimpses into the past. The cafes and gas stations are mostly boarded up, but some of the old motor courts are hanging on. Their rusty welcome signs notwithstanding, my imagination has me convinced that the cars parked there now belong to those more interested in "getting around" than traveling.

Winding Roads, Lonely Roads

The early morning ride north on Route 11/15 is another easy jaunt away from the city, especially when riding against rush-hour traffic. The weather-beaten buildings lining the old riverside road hint at a colorful history that, like the Susquehanna, swirls and eddies around every bend. Route 849, winding out of Duncannon, proves to be a much nicer wake-up call than more static and tinny warbling from some "American Idol" also-ran, too. From the moment the pavement begins to twist its way up and out of the river valley, it's obvious that I need to be on the ball. The Harley and I begin our traffic-free tango, negotiating a plethora of smooth, snaking bends. Turning north outside Newport allows a small breather with a relaxing ride along the Juniata River, but after a quick right on Upper Perry Valley Road, which merges with 1010, it's on again. From farms to forests and back to farms again, the rolling pavement twists and turns, inviting a delightfully brisk pace. Through the villages of Seven Stars,

Maze, and Cocolamus the Harley thumps and jumps unwaveringly. On this loop, keep an eye on the fuel supply. Despite being awarded spots on the state highway map, most of these boroughs end up being little more than a cluster of houses and maybe a boarded-up general store with a faded gas pump that has probably been dry since the Arab oil embargo.

By the time I reach Van Wert, destination signs are more prevalent than route numbers. I begin following the surprisingly accurate arrows to the next town on the route. Bounding across Route 74, I'm heading straight into a mountain. The next several miles ascend and fall through thick stands of hardwoods that allow brief expansive views of the valleys below. But a deer springing across the road startles me into a heightened state of concentration, eyes scanning the road ahead and the woods nearby.

After a brief rendezvous with Route 17 in Ickesburg, I follow the arrow for Saville. This proves to be a good call as the town's covered bridge, built in 1903, is still in service. Riding across one of these relics is a delight that never falls out of fashion. Joining Route 274, I soon plunge into the Big Spring State Forest. The number of hunting lodges and "hunt safely" signs is yet another reminder of the need to maintain a sane pace in Bambi-land.

I find my way east on Route 75 through the picture-postcard village of Blairs Mills and back south into another lonely valley. These roads are definitely "locals only" and I love it. The light wind, warm sunshine, and staccato rhythm of the big V-twin are my only companions, and finer friends a man cannot have.

Eastbound on Route 641, the V's lazy beat switches back to rock and roll as "The Twist" begins again over another mountain range. Pegs gouging pavement and a constant grin mark the characteristics of the ride here. Unlike the extended riding highs delivered by romps through the Rockies or the Alps, Appalachian passes hit

↻ *The twists hit hard and fast in the Keystone State.*

with an amphetamine blast: quick, intense, and they leave you wanting more. The pegs are still steaming when I'm guided, as if by magic, to the parking lot of the Path Valley Family Restaurant in Spring Run. If a grilled cheese sandwich with a side of eavesdropping on the ladies disseminating local gossip doesn't bring you back down to earth, nothing will. And if I was a mite younger and not already hitched, I'd probably like to meet Iris's granddaughter. Hear tell she's the prettiest girl at Shippensburg State and a star athlete to boot.

Back underway on Route 75, I swing a right in Fannettsburg toward Burnt Cabins for another hit off the pass pipe. Oooh, I like this stuff. A quick left after cresting a rise has me heading into Cowans Gap State Park. All day long there has been next to no traffic and I soon discover where everyone is. The lake in the park is absolutely packed. Swimmers and picnickers all around. While lamenting the fact that I didn't bring along my swimming trunks, I wonder why all these people aren't at work. Next time I'll have my swim gear on-board and leave my hypocrisy in the motel room.

Motoring back north, I turn the other way in Fannettsburg, heading for another mountaintop. Along with the usual twists and turns, this particular stretch is a perfect study in how not to grade a road. As best I can tell, the construction budget must have been really tight: the guys who built this byway just cut down some trees and laid the asphalt, apparently without leveling the roadbed. The vertical curves are just as intense as the horizontal ones and, on several occasions, the Harley is airborne – in the straightaways! Okay, some of that may have been my doing, but it didn't take much effort. This road is not for

the faint of heart, and I'd advise scheduling a light lunch and an extra half hour. You'll likely want to go back and run this one again.

Route 997 in Roxbury marks the final stretch to Harrisburg. Soon I begin seeing the mileage signs counting me back to town. The day has been long and tiring, but it has certainly been one of the best days of riding I've experienced in quite a while.

Stormy Weather

Nothing throws a wrench into a great tour like an ugly bunch of clouds. I had purposely set the infernal radio for early racket so I could ride down to York and catch the day's first Harley-Davidson Vehicle Operations factory tour. But by the looks of the sky, plans will have to change so I can make some miles before the rain starts.

The temperature is balmy as I point the Super Glide® west. I pick up Route 174 west of Mechanicsburg and swoop along roads traversing more rolling, expansive farmland. Through Boiling Springs and Mount Holly I continue along quiet, traffic-free roads all the way to Shippensburg. Bearing left on Baltimore Road, I head south. This tree-lined road winding a lonely path through the Micheaux State Forest briefly eases my cloudy concerns. Just outside of Arendtsville, a right on Boyer Nursery Road runs me through groves of cherry trees, and the succulent globes hang so near I could reach out and grab a handful.

Turning right on Cashtown Road, I do my best to keep my hopes up as the intermittent patter of rain hits my face shield. The roads maintain their superb character; it's just too bad they're getting a bit damp. In Waynesboro, I notice a number of places to stop for a bite, but I know as soon as

Harley-Davidson Vehicle Operations Factory Tour

No visit to central Pennsylvania is complete without a tour of the Harley-Davidson assembly plant in York. This sprawling facility sits on 230 acres of land and has over 1.5 million square feet under roof. The tours are very well organized and our guide wasn't stumped by a single question the group fired his way. The experience begins in the Vaughn L. Beals Tour Center, a modern building jam-packed with displays and exhibits chronicling the history of the York Vehicle Operations. Then it's off to the production line to watch brand-new Harley-Davidsons materialize. This is the largest of Harley-Davidson's manufacturing facilities and over 3,200 employees work around the clock assembling Touring and Softail® models, as well as limited production factory custom models. Whether your ride of choice happens to be a Hog or a scooter, if you're a two-wheel enthusiast, it's a real treat to see a motorcycle come into being.

The York Vehicle Operations is very easy to find. Simply take Route 30 into town and follow the signs – you can't miss it. Because tour schedules are subject to change, it's advisable to call ahead (877) 883-1450 to make sure something out of the ordinary isn't going on. Production changes and maintenance can result in suspended or abbreviated tours. For more details, visit www.harley-davidson.com and click on Experience.

◗ *Cherry trees line the roadside near Arendtsville.*

I do that I'm in for a legitimate downpour. I must press on.

East of Marion, scooting through the green mountains of the Micheaux State Forest, Route 233 offers up some great twists before settling into a nice peaceful ride through the deep hardwood forest. This would undoubtedly be the most relaxing stretch of the trip were it not for the vigorous pace dictated by the heaviness overhead. Thus far, a few drops causing a little dampness on the knuckles of my gloves and tops of my boots is all the skies have mustered, but I feel as if I'm being stalked.

Taking a right on Route 34, in Hunters Run, closes in on Harrisburg, and I'm a bit heartened, as the drops

have stopped – for now. Afraid to let down my guard, I push on, vowing to keep my raingear stowed. Still dry through Biglerville and Hanover, I roll into York too late for a factory tour. The last sprint begins on Route 181 toward the Susquehanna's western shore. There's very little traffic and it looks like I'm almost home free, that is, until I sneak a peek west. Implacably obliterating most of the visibility in its path, a huge black wall is bearing down on the maroon Harley. As Route 262 turns back toward Interstate 81, a leaden barricade of cold rain hits so suddenly I don't even have time to stop and dig out my slicker. I practically float into the next convenience store, soaked to the skin, not fifteen miles from my warm, dry motel room. Such is the adventure of traveling on

two wheels. I shouldn't complain, though – at least I was spared a drenching in the middle of nowhere. And no matter what, it's still fun to kick back under the awning of a 7-11, munch on a Baby Ruth, and watch it rain.

Despite a somewhat soggy conclusion, I had an incredible experience in the Harrisburg area. The Commonwealth's byways always manage to reward one with challenging rides and relaxing scenery. No matter what you want from a tour, these roads deliver. I've ridden all across the state and have never been disappointed. Pennsylvania may still be one of motorcycling's best kept secrets, and chances are that's the way the riders here like it.

FACTS AND INFORMATION

Total Mileage

Approximately 815 miles.

In General

I've never been disappointed by a ride in the Keystone State. The beautiful scenery, history, and cultural variety tell a different story around every passing corner. From coal trains and Amish buggies to Harleys and Hershey Bars, there's no shortage of fascinating attractions in central Pennsylvania. Unique, handcrafted items can also be found: Everything from quilts to furniture to fresh produce is available in numerous, small, family-run shops.

Travel Season

The weather in Pennsylvania is pleasantly mild throughout the year except for a brief period of snow in the winter and a few rainy months in the beginning of spring. Autumn is a great time to ride, and planning a tour during the second or third week in October will almost guarantee a stunning backdrop of changing leaves.

Roads & Biking

Visit Harrisburg and you'll discover some of the best motorcycling around. The mountain roads north of town offer challenging twisties one minute and soothing swoops the next. For the most part, the tarmac is in surprisingly good shape despite the region's harsh winters. Because there are a number of industrial and mining areas, watch for big trucks and gravel in the corners. Share the road respectfully, especially with Amish buggies in sight.

Maps

○ *Pennsylvania State Highway Map,* available from the Pennsylvania Department of Transportation

More Information

○ Pennsylvania Tourism Office (800) 847-4872 www.visitpa.com
○ Pennsylvania Dutch Convention & Visitors Bureau (800) 723-8824 www.padutchcountry.com

Attractions

❶ Hershey Entertainment and Resorts (800) 437-7439
❷ Yuengling Brewery Tours (570) 622-4141
❸ Harley-Davidson Factory (877) 883-1450
❹ Historic Round Barn & Farm Market (717) 334-1984
❺ Millersburg Ferry (717) 692-2442
❻ Gettysburg National Military Park (717) 334-1124 ext. 8023

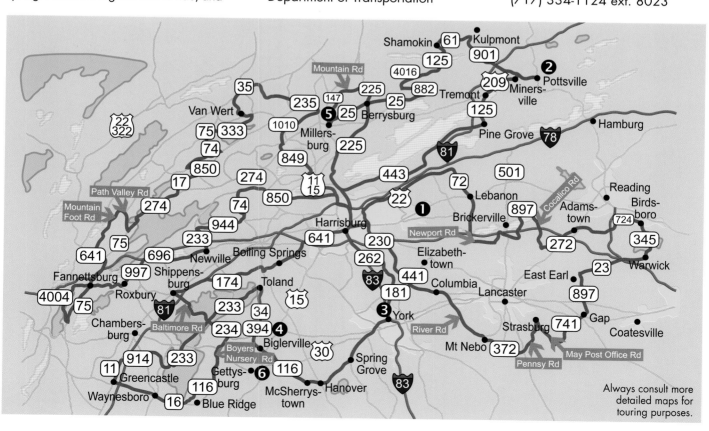

Always consult more detailed maps for touring purposes.

The Northeast

Long Island Scooter Tour
Harbor Hopping in The Hamptons

Long Island, in geological time, was born yesterday. Glaciers that created this 120-mile long, fish-shaped pile of rock and sand began retreating some 22,000 years ago. Sea levels rose in concert with the thaw, completely encircling the land mass 11,000 years later. Today, it's one of the most densely populated areas in America, home to more than 7.5 million people, and Suffolk County, in the easternmost section, is now the recreational playground of choice for many affluent New Yorkers.

Text: James T. Parks
Photography: James and Karen Parks

Sag Harbor

Sagaponack Harbor, or Sag Harbor as it's known today, teemed with people and ships from exotic locations in the 1800s, with the volume of its shipping activity rivaling that of the port of New York. Because of its central location in Suffolk County, charming ambiance and 300 years of history, Karen and I make Sag Harbor our home base for touring "The Hamptons" and other points of interest. Early on a clear and cool summer morning, we launch our Long Island road adventure on the Kymco Xciting 500cc scooter.

Powerboats and sailboats dot the seascape of Sag Harbor and its bay, and while cruising down Main Street, I immediately notice the expensive automobiles parked on the street: Ferrari, Maserati, Porsche, Bentley... And when

➲ *East Hampton tranquility.*

↻ *The stately, refurbished movie palace in Westhampton Beach.*

pulling onto the pier, we're treated to even grander displays of excess in the squadron of private yachts arrayed in the harbor. The Kymco scooter certainly won't be turning any heads in this well-heeled community, but we're quite happy with its park-anywhere versatility and motorcycle-like handling, not to mention its gas-sipping proclivity.

Shelter Island

North on SR 114, there's an expansive view from a bridge of Noyack Bay. South Ferry takes us across to Shelter Island, which, as the name implies, shelters the Peconic Bays from the open sea to the east. The first Europeans settling this island in the 1600s were wealthy sugar merchants from Barbados, who harvested

◐ *Montauk Point Lighthouse: "Protecting mariners since 1797."*

the stands of white oak trees primarily for shipping barrels. The year-round population of the island today is about 2,500 residents. Continuing on SR 114, the ride becomes curvier and the traffic lighter. The kickstand drags on a fast left-hander, but the fun is over all too soon when the North Ferry gate comes into view.

North Fork Wine Country

There are more than 20 vineyards on Long Island and most are located in the ideal weather and soil conditions of the North Fork. Many of them offer tours and winetastings in their facilities.

We pull off the road to visit Duck Walk Vineyards and, after the tour, buy a bottle of blush for consumption later. It's now past noon, but none of the restaurants on SR 25 strike our fancy, so we dash south to The Hamptons.

The Hamptons

Beach communities situated along the South Fork include Westhampton Beach, Hampton Bays, Bridge Hampton, Southampton, and East Hampton. Some of the villages are larger than the others, but all of them seem to have one thing in common: quaint shops selling very expensive merchandise.

Stopping in Westhampton Beach, we're soothed by cool Atlantic breezes as we enjoy a delicious salmon sandwich on the Margarita Grille's patio. A tranquil scene unfolds before us on Main Street: shoppers stroll lazily along the tree-lined sidewalks, occasionally stopping to peer into the windows, and convertibles filled with beachgoers cruise by in search of empty parking spots. From our table we can see The Westhampton, a beautifully restored movie palace that's still showing first-run movies. Revived, we remount and ride through one Hampton village after another, each with its own assemblage of incredibly tony shops.

🎧 *Anticipatory musings: Karen, on the ferry to the North Fork of Long Island.*

🎧 *A nice little beach cottage in East Hampton.*

Karen squirms on the back seat, twisting left and right to note all of the shopping opportunities, but I keep the scooter tracking at a steady pace and feign hearing loss in an effort to delay the inevitable stop to shop. My strategy works, but it succeeds only because our schedule is too tight today for a prolonged stop. Undoubtedly, I'll pay for it later.

As might be expected, many of the houses in the Hamptons are built on a grand scale. We photograph a particularly stunning home in East Hampton and, taking a breather by a pond across the street, we watch a child and his mother feed baby geese as a swan glides regally by on the smooth surface.

On to Montauk Point

To the east, the South Fork becomes narrower until it's less than a mile wide in some locations. The village of Montauk was named for the Native Americans who lived in the area long before the first Europeans arrived in the early sixteenth century.

Most of the land on the eastern tip of the South Fork of Long Island has been protected from development, and riding through the remoteness of its heavy vegetation provides a nice escape from the hubbub close by in the concrete jungles. The beach at Ditch Plaines is considered the epicenter of the East Coast surfing scene, with many drawn here to test their skills. A little farther down SR 27, where the road literally ends, visitors also come to enjoy the most iconic image of Long Island.

Construction of the Montauk Point Lighthouse was approved by none other than President George Wash-

⌐ *A fishing vessel enters Montauk Harbor with the catch of the day.*

ington in 1792. When completed in 1797 on the spit of land where Long Island Sound meets the Atlantic Ocean, the lighthouse was over 300 feet from the water's edge. However, erosion over the ensuing years shrank the distance to only 50 feet. Giorgina Reid, a modern-day heroine, dedicated many years of her life to terracing the hillside location of the lighthouse, arresting further depletion of the land at Montauk Point. The Montauk Historical Society also keeps a careful watch over the lighthouse and museum in the former keeper's quarters (both open to the public) to help ensure their preservation for the enjoyment of future generations.

Turned around and heading west into the setting sun, we stop briefly at Montauk Harbor to view the many pleasure craft under sail in Fort Pond Bay and the commercial fishing vessels returning with their day's catch. A man on one of the boats proudly holds up a large fish for other crewmembers to admire. Continuing west on SR 27, we soon turn north in East Hampton onto the twisting path of SR 114 for the final few miles back to Sag Harbor.

Tour's End

To celebrate a wonderful time, we splurge on a first-class dinner at The American Hotel in Sag Harbor. With fresh seafood so close at hand, it's no wonder all of our meals on this tour have been so delicious. The fine cuisine and alfresco ambiance at The American Hotel make a fitting end to a great day of touring.

A cool, dry breeze wafts down Main Street as dusk falls on old Sag Harbor. And there's no doubt in our minds that the east end of Long Island is a wonderful place to spend a day, a week, a month – or a lifetime.

Long Island, New York
FACTS AND INFORMATION

Total Mileage

Approximately 120 miles.

In General

Suffolk County, New York, with its two forks of land enclosing a large bay, is located at the easternmost section of Long Island. The Hamptons, on the South Fork, are beach communities with numerous upscale shops along the main streets. Sag Harbor and the other communities located on harbors in the bays have a definite nautical flavor. The North Fork of Suffolk County is wine country. This tour is best experienced as a leisurely cruise with frequent stops to enjoy the scenery, dining, and shopping. It took us an entire day to cover 120 miles.

Travel Season

Long Island has warm, humid summers and cold winters, making spring and fall the best times for touring here.

Roads & Biking

The roads are in good condition and not heavily traveled, except for the main arteries (SR 27 on the South Fork and SR 25 on the North Fork) in and out of Suffolk County. State Road 27 can be particularly crowded in the afternoon. East, after Amagansett, the traffic on SR 27 is much lighter. Riding all the way out to the Montauk Point Lighthouse is well worth the trip. Because of the high speed of traffic and blind curves on SR 25, pulling onto and off the road can be hazardous – so be extra careful along the North Fork. Crossing Shelter Island on SR 114, to reach either of the forks, necessitates two short, but scenic ferry rides. There are many interesting side loops off the main route to explore if time permits.

Maps

o *New York State Atlas & Gazetteer*
DeLorme
ISBN 0899332579, $19.95

More Information

o Cross Sound Ferry Services, Inc.
(860) 443-5281
(Long Island & New England)
www.longislandferry.com
o Long Island CVB & Sports Commission
www.licvb.com
o Explore Long Island
www.exploreli.com
o The Hamptons Visitors Council
www.hamptonsvisitorscouncil.com

Attractions

❶ Railroad Museum of Long Island
(631) 727-7920
❷ Montauk Point Lighthouse
(631) 668-2544
❸ Home Sweet Home, (631) 324-0713
❹ Sag Harbor Sailing, (631) 725-5100
❺ Camp Hero State Park
(631) 668-3781
❻ Southold Indian Museum
(631) 765-5577
❼ Hallockville Museum, (631) 298-5292

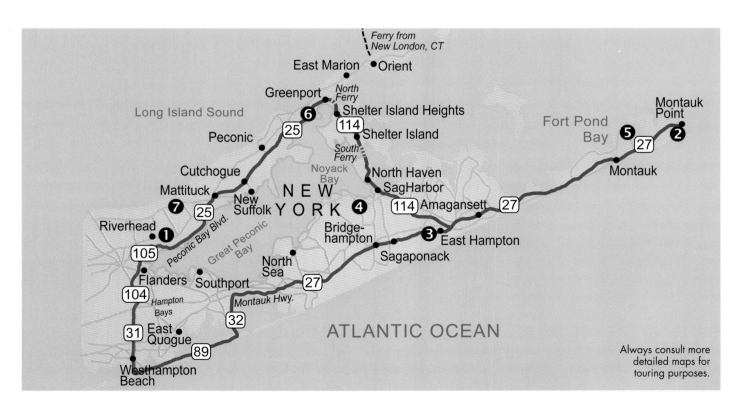

Group Riding

Sharing the experience of the road, the companionship and camaraderie, make riding with others a great deal of fun. And if you do it right, it's safer than riding alone, but if you get it wrong, it can be downright dangerous.

The goal of riding in a group of bikes is to make sure your "danger zone" – the space ahead of you, behind and to the side – is kept clear of other vehicles. You should keep a space of at least two seconds clear directly in front and the same behind, and avoid encouraging other vehicles to share your lane. That includes other motorcycles.

If you've ever seen or followed a group of police motorcyclists, you'll notice they often ride with two bikes side by side in lane. Motorcycle safety organizations, including the MSF, recommend you avoid riding alongside another bike because it's more dangerous.

Imagine that each lane on the road is divided into three narrower lanes: the left side, the center, and the right side of the lane. In general, it's a good idea to avoid the center of the lane. That's where the "grease strip" lain down by leaky auto engines is, and it's especially treacherous in wet weather. In most situations, you should avoid riding on the grease strip.

So, if you're riding in a group, avoiding the grease strip, not riding side by side and allowing the maximum distance around you, the safest logical option is a "staggered" formation. If the bike in front of you is riding to the left side of the lane, ride to the right side of the lane, and vice versa. You should leave a minimum of one second between you and the rider in front of you, assuming they're on the other side of your lane. That should make you two seconds behind the rider ahead in the same lane position as you are.

(If you're moving from one side of your lane to the other, remember to check your mirrors and shoulder check before switching. Don't use your turn signal: it might confuse other riders.)

Before you set out on a ride with a group, make sure every rider understands these guidelines, and agree on a target speed that will work for everyone. If you keep to a one-second gap, you shouldn't have too many problems with cars pulling in to split the group, but it may happen. Let the car in and give it plenty of room. Slow down if necessary, and don't try to race it. In a collision with a car, you'll always lose.

A couple of other things about groups: as you slow down and stop, the group will inevitably get tighter, with the bikes closer together; and as you accelerate, the group will open out. Make sure you allow for this. Remember that you're no longer acting in isolation. Your actions affect the other riders in the group. Avoid sudden speed and direction changes.

Let's say you're leading the group. Be aware of your pace and that of the riders behind you. Use your mirrors to monitor traffic behind you. And it's important to think ahead. If you see a "stale" green traffic signal ahead, look for telltale signs (like a flashing pedestrian light) that the light is about to change. When changing lanes or passing, allow for the possibility that another rider might follow you regardless of traffic conditions.

If you're riding in the middle of the group, ride your own ride. Don't just blindly follow the rider ahead. Scan the road before you and anticipate just as you would on your own. On narrow twisty roads, or through blind hills or curves, ride in single file and leave extra time to react.

Riding in the back of the group requires that you watch the group leader (or the riders well in front of you) as well as the traffic all around you. If the group is changing or merging lanes, you may want to move early to block the lane from traffic behind. This can prevent cars from getting stuck in the middle of the group. You may also want to choose the "dominant" lane position, even if it means riding directly behind the bike in front of you. Just leave an extra second's space.

Have fun riding in a group – but stay safe!

MAINE
INTO THOREAU'S WOODS

The biggest, wildest state in New England, Maine is also the first state in the union to catch the light of the rising sun. As a September dawn wakes me in Kennebunkport, the nearby routes along this storied coast exert a very strong pull – nearly 3,500 miles of beaches, bays, inlets, and harbors – but I have other intriguing plans for the day.

Text and Photography: John Flores

◯ *Looking forward to a lot of great roads and views.*

Day 1: Coastal Getaway

I follow US 9 north to Saco, where I catch SR112. Passing under Interstate 95, I leave the lobsters and coast behind. I'm heading inland, to the land of the moose, and the mountains and lakes and woods that begat Paul Bunyan and inspired Thoreau.

SR117 is on my escape route, a quiet road that becomes more rural with each passing mile. As the morning progresses, mountains appear in the distance and small vistas reveal themselves on open stretches. Trees, trees, and more trees, parting only for the numerous lakes or odd farms that dot the countryside. These are the Maine woods, covering 90 percent of the state and standing thick as thieves.

After a mellow morning ride, Bridgton is a good stop for lunch. Like other small towns in the state, Bridgton has an unassuming air and a character all

its own – Ricky's Diner, replete with fifties-era décor and an old jukebox, is next to a leather and tattoo shop with a miniature custom cruiser parked out front.

I stay on SR117 until Buckfield, where I join SR140 north to SR219 west. Pavement flecks flash in the afternoon sun as the road continues to twist and rise. In West Paris, I head teasingly toward the White Mountains of New Hampshire on SR26. They're growing on the horizon, but in Newry I turn on SR2 east and end the temptation. New Hampshire will have to wait. I have more of Maine to see.

I meet the legendary lumberjack Paul Bunyan in Rumford. Other states may claim him as a native son, yet here he stands, over 15 feet tall and towering above the Kawasaki. State lore maintains he and his blue ox Babe were born in Maine, and as loggers traveled west

○ *Patriotic bunting rustles above PegaLeg Pete's in breezy Bridgton.*

they carried tales of the outrageous pair with them. This particular statue of Paul used to greet customers of a local hardware store but was brought to the information center at Rumford Falls when the store closed.

On SR17 in Mexico, ME, I start the final stretch of the day with a sense of urgency, eager to find shelter and a warm meal before the sun sets. The road bisects a farm-lined valley before following a crooked, raging river. Without warning, the road rises, and then rises some more to a breathtaking view of Lake Mooselookmeguntic. A little further along there's an equally stunning twilit view of Rangeley Lake. I ride for moments like this – to be shaken from the stupor of everyday life and renewed by the incomparable beauty in this world.

I reach the town of Rangeley in the fading light. Located halfway between the equator and the North Pole, the town feels like a sleepy vacation outpost,

and much farther from Kennebunkport than the 200 miles and 1,507 feet in altitude change might suggest. The sidewalks are rolled up for the evening except for the ruckus at Sarge's, a country-sports/karaoke bar, if you can imagine that. Some patrons are willing the Red Sox to victory, while others are belting out classic Country/Western tunes. It's a fun way to close out the day.

Day 2: The Wild, Wild East

I leave Rangeley on SR16 after having some strong coffee and a great omelet at the BMC Diner. In Stratton, SR16 turns southeast and passes the Sugarloaf Mountain ski resort before shadowing the Carrabasset River into Kingfield. The mountains fill the mirrors as I climb out of town. Part of the beauty of riding is watching the land transform beneath your wheels and arriving at places where that transformation is projected in sharp relief. Kingfield is one of those places. East of town the land flattens and in fifteen minutes the mountains are gone.

For me, a resident of New Jersey (the most densely populated state in the nation), Maine (the least densely popu-

○ *This stalwart beast stands guard at Moosehead Lake.*

⟳ *Dusk descends on Rangeley Lake.*

lated state east of the Mississippi River) feels desolate. Towns are miles apart and usually defined by little more than an intersection and a small collection of weathered homes. Maybe there's a gas station and convenience store. In between you'll roam miles and miles of wild that but for the road appear untouched by man, the way I thought it only existed out West or to the north in the Canadian woods.

I find gas and lunch on SR201 in Solon and watch life go by as the late-summer sun takes the edge off the early autumn chill. Refueled, I continue along the Kennebec River, the land and sky expanding in my field of vision as I head north towards the Canadian border. The next "big" town, Jackman (pop. 712), is nearly 50 miles away, leaving just me, the logging trucks that run this road and a Canadian racing for the border in an SUV. The Kawasaki devours the generous sweepers, the long arrow-straight climbs on the hills, and the flat sections where the vista extends for miles. The logging trucks aren't doing that badly either, their drivers confidently pushing the rigs. Frost heaves and patchy pavement keep my top speed in check while the Canadian's dogged persistence keeps him a dot in the mirrors – sometimes growing, sometimes shrinking, but always there.

From Jackman, I head east on SR6 toward Moosehead Lake, the largest lake in Maine, and feel even more isolated. No more logging trucks, no more high-speed Canadians – just me, the bike, and the woods. It's easy to be charmed by their quiet splendor, and I know that I'm not the first to feel this way. The naturalist Henry David Thoreau wandered these woods alone too, canoeing and hiking, and climbing Mt. Kineo, the shear, flinty prominence that rises 700 improbable feet above the lake's surface.

◑ *The Kawasaki devours another ridge in the woods of Maine.*

But before the mountain, I take a detour down an active logging road in search of the Katahdin Iron Works. In its heyday (the mid-1800s), the Iron Works produced 2,000 tons of pig iron a year with the help of 200 men, 16 charcoal kilns, and a towering blast furnace. A small company town and railroad grew from this venture, but all that remain six miles down a gravel road are the shell of the blast furnace and a lone charcoal kiln.

I return to asphalt and continue towards Mt. Katahdin. SR11 stretches to Millinocket, where I follow the signs to Baxter State Park. The mountain looms larger by the minute: a small feature on the horizon this morning has become an imposing, hulking mass. Suddenly, Katahdin disappears. I've entered Baxter State Park and the road shrinks – tight, winding, and covered by a thick canopy of limbs and leaves that blot out the sky. This is as close as I'll get. As part of its original intent, to remain "forever wild," the park is closed to motorcycles. And as wild as the landscape has been to now, even this brief glimpse of Baxter exceeds it, feeling even more primitive and dark. The thick woods seem ready to swallow the sun and any hints of man's presence.

Leaving the mountain behind, I stop to examine the mural on a huge, garage-sized boulder. First painted in the 1970s by high-school students, the mural is a panorama of forest life, showing a bear beside a raging brook, a fish leaping upstream, and a deer looking off into the distance. Geese fly overhead near Katahdin, and above them the words "Keep Maine Beautiful" float in the sky. Two local artists, Abbot and Nancy, have restored the mural a few times before, and here they are again on a bright September day, giving their time to preserve the sentiments of Thoreau and others who have visited the Maine woods and been similarly awed.

Moosehead Lake is a tranquil giant, 120 square miles of secluded coves and bays punctuated by 80 forested islands. A handful of late-season vacationers quietly ply the waters, as though mindful of the mystical mood. I desperately want to stay awhile, settle on a porch somewhere and just stare at the mountain and lake in the changing light. But with dusk approaching I have many miles to go, and continue down SR6, racing again to find a room. Greenville, Guilford, and Dover-Foxcroft are dispatched with a twist of the wrist, and a warm bed, clean bath, and hot meal are found in Milo.

Day 3: Keep Maine Beautiful

Figuratively and literally, the morning is dominated by another mountain – Mt. Katahdin. The northern terminus of the Appalachian Trail and the jewel of Baxter State Park, it soars dramatically over its flat surround much like Kilimanjaro in Tanzania and Ayer's Rock/Uluru in Australia. I ride up SR11 to get as close as I can.

I stop in Millinocket for lunch and roll on. SR11 turns left and SR157 continues ahead, crossing Interstate 95. I pause. By crossing I-95, I'll be leaving the Maine of the moose and returning to the Maine of the lobster. I'm not ready. I turn around and turn north on SR11 in Medway. The road borders a small creek for awhile and then rises. Over my left shoulder, Katahdin guards the western horizon, shadowing my progress for a few more precious miles before I give in, turn east, and cross I-95 on SR158.

The land, rolling and tilting softly, eventually flattening, is hatch-marked with more intersecting roads, farms and houses and traffic than I've seen altogether in the past few days. SR158 blends into SR2 south, which flows into SR2A south. They're fine country roads but they elicit little excitement. Maybe it's the drag of another long day. Maybe it's what's behind, the magic of the Maine woods... SR170 south begets SR169 south begetting SR6 east where the final folds of earth unfurl onto the sea-level plain.

On US 1 South I join a line of cars bound for Calais. I refuel there and consider stopping for the evening. But I've been spoiled – and even in my fatigued state, the idea of spending an evening here holds little appeal. I decide to press on a bit further south and wearily drag myself into Robbinston, as far as I can safely go. The drab motel and cramped room make me feel like a caged animal. Fresh mountain air has been replaced with the pungent odor of chemical cleaning products. I open all the windows for relief, eat a simple meal, and fall asleep to the sound of the receding tide.

Day 4: Final Surprise

I awaken to morning fog – and construction. The ZX-14 soldiers on, its prodigious horsepower held in check

↻ *Making a beeline for Mt. Katahdin.*

↺ *Abbot and Nancy spruce up another patch of Maine for future generations.*

⋂ Mooselookmeguntic Lake looks like paradise.

as I ride on patches of soft soil. My breakfast is served at the WaCo Diner in Eastport, the easternmost diner in the easternmost settlement in the U.S. It's a popular spot for watching the surging waters of Passamaquoddy Bay (an inlet of the Bay of Fundy noted for its massive tidal swings), including the Old Sow, the largest tidal whirlpool in the Western Hemisphere.

It's raining and cold when I leave Eastport. I tuck my gauntlets into my sleeves and shove off. There's not going to be a lot to see in this meteorological soup, so I make my way to US 9 (via 214, 191, and Cooper Road) on a beeline for Bangor. I'm so focused on the road that I barely notice the spare beauty of the rolling, desolate terrain. It's a tough slog – I'm still fatigued and chilled to boot – using the velocity of the Kawasaki to keep safe gaps between myself and others. I'm not the only nut on the road though: other bikers are pressing onward in the opposite direction.

Bangor brings relief. The showers abate. I catch US 1 South, and all of the traffic and development come as a slight shock to the system after days of solitude. Fleeting glimpses of the sea float by as

I focus on today's lunch stop in Camden, a charming little town, with lots of shops and people out on a Saturday afternoon. And it's worth the trip for Cappy's Chowder House alone, a great recommendation I owe to a virtual friend.

The last miles dwindling, I think the trip is over, the highlights logged, the cameras put away; but I'm in for one final treat by taking SR105 from downtown Camden. As I head inland with Mt. Battie over my right shoulder, the

pavement is drying, and the road becomes a quirky collection of dips, rises, and apexes all the way to Augusta. All that's left now is a short ride back to Kennebunkport.

Strangely, in my four days of wandering, I didn't run across a single moose – the closest I got was a black cat in Rangeley. But I was able to linger awhile in the woods and by the waters Thoreau found so mesmerizing, and wouldn't be surprised if, like him, I found myself visiting them once more. 🄳

🄳 The sun sets on another glorious day of riding.

Maine
FACTS AND INFORMATION

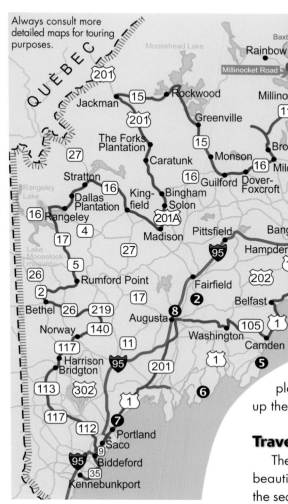

Always consult more detailed maps for touring purposes.

Northern Maine contains many dirt roads that invite exploration with a dual purpose/adventure touring bike, but most of the roads on this trip can be ridden on anything from a standard to a tourer.

Maps
○ *Maine Atlas & Gazetter*, Delorme ISBN 089933282X, $19.95
○ *Moto Map of Maine* www.greatroadsgreatrides.com $9.95

More Information
○ www.visitmaine.com
○ www.maineguide.com

Attractions
❶ Old Sow Whirlpool Survivor's Association (207) 853-2922
❷ Fort Halifax (207) 941-4014
❸ Baxter State Park (207) 723-5140
❹ Katahdin Scenic Cruises (207) 723-2020
❺ Owls Head Light State Park (207) 941-4014
❻ Pemaquid Point Light (207) 677-2494
❼ Downeast Duck (207) 774-3825
❽ Old Fort Western (207) 626-2385
❾ Fort O'Brien State Historic Site (207) 941-4014

Total Mileage
Approximately 983 miles.

In General
Maine is the biggest state in New England, with short summers and long winters. Much of the inland recreation revolves around outdoor activities (hunting, fishing, kayaking, and hiking). It's the least densely populated state east of the Mississippi, so most roads are lightly traveled, except in tourist areas during the summer and fall foliage seasons.

Over half of the state consists of "unorganized territories" with no local government. If you're thinking about exploring out-of-the-way regions of Maine, plan ahead. The small towns roll up their sidewalks early.

Travel Season
The summers are short but extremely beautiful in Maine, especially along the seashore where gusty winds break up the humidity. For this reason, tourists flock here during the months of July and August when the average temperature is in the mid-seventies. To avoid large crowds and over-priced hotels and restaurants, try to visit late in the season. Mild and quiet, September is a good time for touring.

Roads & Biking
A Maine winter is harsh, and logging trucks are heavy, hulking beasts. The combination very often damages the road surface, quickly changing it from billiard-table smooth to frost-heaved and heavily patched. Look far ahead, up the road, and pass logging trucks with care.

How it all started

History of *RoadRUNNER Motorcycle Touring & Travel* magazine:

In the summer of 1999, Christian and Christa Neuhauser moved from Austria to North Carolina with their two teenage sons. This was a natural step, progressing from the many weeks spent traveling in the US, through 42 of its states. They were hooked on motorcycling. It was their preferred means of getting around, and Christian would spend hours, even days, studying maps to discover "new" riding areas.

Their passion for riding and traveling coalesced into the creation of *RoadRUNNER* magazine. As newcomers in this part of the world, they had a clear idea of what readers wanted: a magazine that reflected their passion for riding, the allure of roads less traveled, and memorable destinations. They gathered an ambitious team to bring their idea to life and refused to compromise in any meaningful way on their vision for the magazine's production. *RoadRUNNER* was going to be a magazine of the highest quality filled with entertaining, informative touring articles and outstanding photography.

The first issue of *RoadRUNNER* came out in 2001. Today, it's a unique publication firmly established in the American motorcycle world, in which the magazine enjoys widespread support from both readers and the motorcycle industry in general.

Christian Neuhauser died in a motorcycle accident in 2005. Nevertheless, his wife, Christa, continued building upon their shared vision for the magazine and the family's undaunted enthusiasm for motorcycle touring. She is supported in this endeavor by her two sons, Manuel and Florian, and has a committed team by her side. This book is dedicated to the memory of Christian Neuhauser, an extraordinary motorcycle enthusiast and industry visionary, the founder of *RoadRUNNER Motorcycle Touring & Travel* magazine.

www.RoadRUNNER.travel

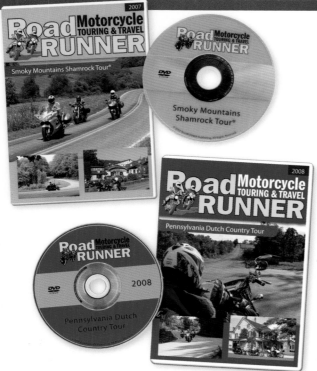